HOW TO WRITE ESSAYS

HOW TO WRITE ESSAYS

Roger Lewis

Heinemann
in association with the National Extension College

Heinemann Educational Books Ltd
22 Bedford Square, London WC1B 3HH

LONDON EDINBURGH MELBOURNE AUCKLAND
HONG KONG SINGAPORE KUALA LUMPUR NEW DELHI
IBADAN NAIROBI JOHANNESBURG
EXETER (NH) KINGSTON PORT OF SPAIN

ISBN 0 435 10499 3

© National Extension College 1976, 1979
First published 1976
by the National Extension College

This revised edition
first published by Heinemann
Educational Books Ltd 1979
Reprinted 1982

Printed in Great Britain by
Biddles Ltd, Guildford, Surrey

CONTENTS

Guide to The Course: Your Questions Answered 1

Unit 1 Tackling the Essay-Writing Task 4

Unit 2 Types of Essay and How to Collect Material 12

Unit 3 Making the Outline Plan 31

Unit 4 Practical Matters: Presentation 45

Unit 5 Putting It All Together: Writing a Complete Essay 61

Unit 6 Learning From Essays 76

Discussions 86

Bibliography 104

GUIDE TO THE COURSE

Your Questions Answered

1. Is this the course for me?

Whatever their previous education, many students find essay writing difficult – even those who already have degrees. If you feel *your* essay technique needs improving then this course is for you. Basically, all you need to begin with is a will to learn.

2. Do I need to be able to write good English?

In general, the course assumes an ability to write English with reasonable fluency. If you find this difficult you should perhaps first try a course in 'O' Level English Language (e.g. *A New English Course* by Rhodri Jones, Heinemann Educational Books). There is a section on 'expression' but this essay-writing course is unable to go into such things as spelling and punctuation in depth.

3. What should I learn from the course?

By the end of the course you should be able to tackle essays of any kind with confidence. In particular you should be able to do the following things:

- Understand the question you have to answer
- Collect the material for it
- Sort out material relevant to the question
- Make a plan from this material
- Write the essays, using the plan as your outline
- Learn from your teacher's comments on the essay.

4. How is this course different from others?

There have been many books which include sections on essay writing. But this is a course which tries *to involve you* at all points in learning the skills. *You* should be active throughout.

5. What is an 'essay'?

One definition runs – 'a continuous piece of writing . . . varying in length from at least 500 words (usually about 2–3 quarto sides of paper) to about 5000 words for a special essay'. (The longest essay on this course will be 1500 words.)

6. Will the course be helpful if I have to write up projects, or write papers?

Yes. 'Essay' is really being used as a shorthand word for all kinds of continuous writing. The essay is still the commonest form of writing in education, but slowly it is losing ground to such forms as the 'project', 'report' or 'paper'. This is because education increasingly takes more account of the 'real world' – few people write essays as part of their jobs. Yet we might well have write in connected paragraphs. Our aim here is to look at features common to all such writing.

7. How should I tackle this course?

You'll soon see that the course contains lots of *questions*. These require you to stop, think, and to write something down. It is very important to answer these questions, as they are there to help you to learn for yourself. It is *tempting* to read on – but don't. The course aims at involving you in a conversation with the author, with your own voice heard throughout. After a while, you should get used to this, and enjoy being active.

   You will need a pencil and notebook to keep a full record of your answers and commentary. Use the questions as a further opportunity to write good English: take your time over expressing your ideas in your notebook. The questions will also, we hope, make you think, and thinking is something you have to do at every stage of writing an essay.

0.1

When you see this symbol, pause and write down your answer in your notebook. (The question number will be written in the symbol.)

Discussion: Each question is carefully examined in a **Discussion** which looks at possible answers to the question, ways of tackling it, and important points to consider. These appear at the back of the book (starting on page 86) and you should make sure that you have answered the question fully before you turn to the relevant **Discussion**.

Study the Discussion section carefully. Some of the questions will have 'right' answers. Most, though, are matters of emphasis and opinion and you must not feel worried if you disagree slightly with the author. Try to see why, and if you disagree strongly discuss it with your teacher.

8. Should I read the course through first?

You might like to skim the course – look over it quickly – before starting to work through it in the way suggested above. This will help you to see how the Units fit together. But don't look too closely at the question and answers.

9. Do I need any other books?

The course is self-contained and you don't need any extra books other than a good dictionary (see below). Further reading is suggested for students needing more practice or advice and you should be putting your essay-writing skills into practice in the other subjects you are studying.

You should have a good dictionary. This should be modern: the *Concise Oxford Dictionary* (OUP) and *Chambers' Twentieth Century Dictionary* (Chambers) are both good. So is the *Penguin Dictionary* (Penguin) and the *Heinemann English Dictionary* (Heinemann Educational Books). You should use your dictionary to check on the meanings of new words you meet and on their spellings.

10. Do I need a teacher?

You can follow this course on your own but it will be most useful if you can study it with help. The work you carry out in the assignments should, if at all possible, be commented on by a teacher.

UNIT 1

Tackling the Essay-Writing Task

1. Things to look for
2. You can learn to write essays
3. We use essay-writing skills in speaking
4. Moving from speaking to writing
5. Assignment A
6. Revision exercises

1 Things to Look For

When you have worked through this Unit and carried out the related activities, you should be able to:

● See how essay writing is a skilled activity, like many other activities you do every day.

● Realise that *you* can learn the essay-writing skills.

● Be more aware of the skills you use every day in your speaking, and see how these relate to essay writing.

● See some of the differences between communicating by speaking and communicating by writing.

● Identify the particular difficulties presented by writing.

● Realise that, by working through the exercises and the assignment, you will have started to practise your own writing.

● Feel much more confident about tackling essay writing.

2 You Can Learn to Write Essays

Each day we carry out many skilled activities, though we may not be aware of doing so. Even tying a shoelace and boiling an egg come into this category. List as many such activities as you can think of in 5 minutes.

We can take each of these activities and divide it into three parts:

● Knowledge

4

- Skills

- Attitude

To take one of the examples I gave, we can list these parts of tying a shoelace:

Knowledge: you have to know that you thread an end of the lace through the eyelet of the shoe.
Skill: you need a certain control over your hand movements.
Attitude: you must *want* to tie the lace and be willing to put up with the bending and fiddling involved.

1.1
List the knowledge, skills and attitude you need in order to boil an egg.

Write down the knowledge, skills and attitude needed to carry out one of the activities you listed under Section 2. It's interesting to see how wide-ranging the knowledge, skills and attitudes are in our everyday life, e.g. in getting to school, doing a job in the house, or playing a sport. When we're used to doing something we tend to take for granted the range of abilities involved in doing it.

Essay writing, too, is a combination of *knowledge*, *skill* and *attitude*. We need to have something to say (knowledge), the ability to write English (skill) and – very important – the *confidence* to tackle the job (attitude). Attitude might have seemed relatively insignificant in the examples of the shoelace and the egg. In essay writing, though, it really matters, and you will see how it is stressed throughout this course.

In our everyday life we use skills very like those involved in writing an essay. Take cooking a meal. In this task, there is quite a lot of **planning** and **decision-making** involved. If you are working from a recipe you have to understand the terms used in cookery. You have to know which ingredients go together and how and when to mix them. You have to plan a cooking sequence, e.g. the potatoes go on half an hour before the joint is ready. Similar skills are needed in essay writing where, as we shall see, we have to:

- *Decide* what we are going to do.

- *Collect* together our materials. (Not pots and pans now but ideas, feelings and facts.)

- *Plan* the structure of our essay.

- *Write* our essay.

You might be asking, 'This is all very well, but can you teach me to write good essays?' You would probably agree that most people could do many of the things you listed earlier, given helpful teaching. It is the same with essays; you *can* do a workmanlike job if you are helped to see what skills are involved.

Look back over your list. Can you remember how you learned to do those things? Jot down your answer before moving on.

You will probably find that someone helped you to learn most of them – even if only by letting you watch and then experiment for yourself.

We have to be helped to learn most things – few skills 'come naturally'. I know that I couldn't cook successfully unless someone helped me to learn the necessary skills. I might muddle along on my own, but I should probably waste a lot of time.

The skills used in writing essays apply whatever the subject – clear thinking, lucid writing, ability to group relevant points together, and so on. Certainly, I find as a teacher that I have to draw attention to such general skills very frequently. My students often have plenty of good ideas but they find it difficult to organise them on paper.

Some teachers assume that essay-writing skills are 'picked up' anyway by students. But I feel that this approach does not work for many of us. Could you pick up the technique of successful golf, canoeing, or bridge without any help? Could many children learn to read just by being left alone with a book? Even if learning did occur under such circumstances, it would be very wasteful of time and energy.

Think back through your schooldays. Have you been taught essay-writing skills as such? If you have, then you are luckier than I was. Some teachers did give some help, incidentally, while teaching their subjects. But I can't remember anyone teaching these skills in an organised way.

Do you enjoy writing essays? If so, what subjects do you enjoy writing about?

Only *you* can answer that question. I must say that I found much essay writing difficult and often tedious. I rarely looked forward to writing an essay (except for English essays of an imaginative kind) – do you?

I hope to show in this course how essay-writing is both something which you can learn *and* (very important) something you can enjoy!

3 We Use Essay-Writing Skills in Speaking

Essay titles ask you to do a variety of things:

    'Outline . . .'
    'Narrate . . .'
    'Explain . . .'

We do all these things in our daily lives – though by speaking rather than writing.

Try the following exercise.

1.2
Remind yourself of the last few days and make a list of the occasions when you have been involved in speaking continuously to somebody for a few minutes, whether at home or at work. Try to be as specific as possible, and note the content or aim of the conversation, e.g. 'explained to a friend how to put up the tent I lent him', 'discussed with my father how to grow vegetables'.

4 Moving From Speaking to Writing: Giving Directions

The Spoken Directions

Let us take this further. Many essays require you to *explain* something – the causes of a war, an idea, the process and significance of an experiment, a landscape, etc. Can you think of any *explanations* you have recently given verbally (i.e. by speaking)? You have almost certainly given directions to someone: e.g. explained to them how to get from A to B.

1.3
Do the following things, and write down your answers to each part of the question. (You will have to spend longer on this than on any previous question.)

(a)   Describe the route from your house to the nearest post office, pillar box, telephone kiosk, or bus stop as if someone had asked you. Give this first of all in spoken form, e.g. 'Turn up the road . . .', mentioning any helpful landmarks. (Your directions should allow for several to be mentioned.)
(b)   Now put this into dialogue form with the person you have in mind asking questions or making comments (as he would do in real life). For example, he'd start the dialogue off by asking you the question in the first place –
'Excuse me, but can you tell me the way . . .' or
'Here mate, I'm lost . . .'
Include in your dialogue (in brackets) any actions either person might make, e.g. pointing up the road. (Note: The person must be physically present – he's not on the telephone – and you can't draw him a map.)

The Spoken Directions Examined

Question 1.3 involved the giving of directions, a kind of *explaining* activity; and it is essentially in spoken form.

1.4
Have a look over your dialogue (and at my example, page 86, if you wish), and jot down those features which are typical of speaking rather than writing.

The Written Directions

In a written communication nearly all the aids mentioned in the **Discussion** of Question 1.2 are either lacking or have to be created very differently. This applies whether the writing is seeking to communicate facts, feelings, or argument. You write because the person is distant from you – that's why you have to write. In education, you're always having to write and so you must learn to communicate clearly on paper. The words on the paper carry the message; those squiggles and shapes are all the reader has to go on.

1.5
To see what this involves, use your original directions (if you weren't satisfied with these, either do the exercise again or use my example on page 86), and put them into written form. Imagine that you're writing to a friend who is visiting the area for the first time, and who will need to find his way along that particular route. (Assume that he can get to the starting point.)

The Written Directions Examined

1.6
What are the differences between the first dialogue, and the second written example?

The work you have done so far will have shown that the mental processes you go through when writing essays are basically the same as those you use in everyday life. So there is nothing to be scared of. It is important to realise, though, that the written way of expressing yourself makes certain demands, and you must work hard to fulfil them.

5 Assignment A

In this Assignment you will be:

● Revising the Unit by trying a similar exercise.

● Making an early start at the 'real thing', on a small scale.

● Encouraged to identify any of the weaknesses you think you may have.

1. In this Unit we looked at the example of direction giving, as an activity of the *explanatory* kind. Take another example and work through the same steps:
(a)   Write a dialogue.
(b)   Then turn it into a written communication for the benefit of someone you don't know well.
(c)   Add your comments on any difficulties you encountered in doing this and mentioning which differences between speech and writing were particularly apparent to you in your example.
   If you are stuck for a subject, here are some examples:
  (i) You are telling someone of an experience you had (e.g. being late for school).
 (ii) You are outlining the steps towards achieving something (e.g. an explanation for a friend who wants to build a kite, or to mend a puncture).
(iii) You are giving someone details of a game, a meeting, or a concert. (These can be purely factual or they can include your own feelings.)
Note: do not spend too long on all of this. Try to choose a *short* task, or section of task – of the length of the example in this Unit. If you try to cover too much then you will spend too much time on it.

2. This is intended as a preparation for the rest of the course, and as a guide for your teacher: write down the main problems you encounter/have encountered/expect to encounter in using written English and in writing essays. You can put this in the form of a list, perhaps numbering the points in order of importance for you. (For example you might write 'I find it hard to think of things to say' or 'my spelling is very poor'.) It will be interesting for you to refer back to this list at the end of the course.

6 Revision Exercises

These questions are not intended to be particularly difficult. The answers may seem self-evident at times but the aim is to encourage you to recall, if possible in an entertaining way, the main points of each Unit. You will find the answers at the end of the Unit (page 10), together with further comments.
   Write your answers down and make sure you refer back to the Unit only *after* trying these for yourself.
1. Some of us need a special essay-writing course because: (choose **two** answers from those listed below).
   (a)   We can acquire the skills subconsciously.

(b) There are certain general skills which we can be made aware of.

(c) We are handicapped by poor techniques or we need to brush up techniques we have already acquired.

(d) To pass an exam in 'Essay Writing' so we can get another 'O' level.

(e) It will help us to become better cooks.

2. Essays are 'special' in that: (choose **two** answers from those listed below).

(a) They are very much more difficult than anything else we do in life.

(b) They are normally written in educational institutions and for academic courses.

(c) We have to make a special effort to do them, and we normally write them on our own.

(d) They involve mysterious skills which we do not exercise in ordinary life.

3. Which **one** of the following statements is true?

(a) This course applies only to essays.

(b) This course aims to help the student develop general skills in the organisation and presentation of any piece of continuous written prose.

4. Which of the following statements is the 'odd one out'?
In speaking to one another we often:

(a) Use facial expression.

(b) Use gesture.

(c) Use the other person's responses to help decide what to say next.

(d) Use words and phrases to help maintain social contact.

(e) Talk non-stop.

5. In writing we *generally* have to: (again, find the 'odd one out').

(a) Use more rather than fewer words.

(b) Use language more impersonally than when speaking.

(c) Aim at constructing a 'form' (or shape).

(d) Use punctuation as a useful way of indicating emphasis.

Answers to Revision Exercises

1. (b) and (c) are correct.
I don't think most of us can acquire the skills in the way suggested by (a). I don't know of any 'O' level in 'Essay Writing'.

2. (b) and (c) are right.
If you look back at the Unit you will find I argue (a) and (d) don't apply.

3. (b) is right. See the Guide to the Course.

4. (e) is the 'odd one out'. *Most* of us don't!
5. (a) is the 'odd one out'. The Unit suggests that we have to select more carefully when writing, and that – all other things being equal – we tend to use fewer words.

UNIT 2

Types of Essay and How to Collect Material

1. Things to look for
2. This Unit and its place in the course
3. Types of essay: language of the subject
4. Types of essay: the readers
5. Creative and analytical essays
6. The creative essay
7. The analytical essay:
     key words
     collection of material: asking questions
     selecting from this material
     arranging and storing your material
8. Summary
9. Assignment B
10. Revision exercises
     Appendix 1: some key words defined

1 Things to Look For

When you have worked through this Unit and carried out the related activities, you should be able to:

● Realise that each 'subject' has its own special language, and that the person for whom you are writing will influence your approach to the essay.

● Distinguish between creative and analytical essays.

● Understand what makes a successful creative essay.

● Generate material yourself for a creative essay.

● Recognise the 'key words' in a question.

● Understand what a question is asking of you, by looking at it carefully.

● Ask yourself questions about an essay title, to guide you in your collection of material for an answer.

- Recognise the importance of careful planning and the recording of your ideas.
- Select from the material you collect.

2 This Unit and Its Place in the Course

I hope that Unit 1 has made you feel more confident about writing essays, and that you are clearer about what is involved in written communication. We shall now look at the writing of an essay by breaking the task down into:

- Collecting information. (Unit 2)
- Organising this into an outline plan. (Unit 3)
- Writing up the essay from the outline plan. (Unit 4)
- Consolidating the work you have done, by looking carefully at your teacher's comments, and acting on them where necessary. (Unit 6)

Before we go on, it is important to stress the role of thinking in *all* these stages. Students often hurry to get something down on paper, without stopping to think. Remember:
    Think before you write, read, or take notes.
    Think while you do it.
    Think after you've done it.

3 Types of Essay: Language of the Subject

One important preliminary point: essays can be of many different types. A 'good' essay in one subject (say, English) might be less successful when judged by the criteria of, say, biology. Each subject speaks its own language, as you can see by picking up any textbook.

As a student, you have to learn the language of your subject, and find out what is appropriate when writing about it. Before you start collecting material, you must have assessed correctly the type of essay that is expected of you.

2.1
Read the following three extracts from textbooks. Say which subject is concerned in each case (e.g. 'physics').

With the exception of reflexive verbs and a few verbs expressing motion, French verbs form their Perfect tense (e.g. I have given or I gave) by adding their past participle to the present tense of *avoir*.

The answers to questions 3 and 4 illustrate that if we multiply each side of an equation by the same number, we obtain another equation with the same solution set as the first, i.e. an *equivalent* equation.

Nearly all plants and animals have one characteristic in common. They are made up of cells. If any structures from plants or animals are examined microscopically, they will be seen to consist of more or less distinct units – cells – which, although too small to be seen with the naked eye, in their vast numbers make up the structure of organs.

4 Types of Essay: The Readers

It is not only the subject which determines written style. The writer has also to take into account the interests and attitudes of his readers. You can check this for yourself by looking at any bookstall, and seeing how magazines dealing with the same topic (e.g. cars) differ from one another.

2.2
Read these four extracts, which all deal with books for children. When you have read them through, answer the following questions about each: (i) **What kind of reader do you think it is aimed at?** e.g. doctors, grandparents. (A one word answer will do.) (ii) **How can you tell this from the content and/or the way language is used?** (A sentence will be enough.) Answer both questions for each extract.

(a)   Special Review – Naomi Lewis tells you about *A Wizard of Earthsea* by Ursula Le Guin.
Not many days ago, a remarkable book appeared at my door. If it had come by broomstick or journey-spell it would not be surprising, for it is a tale of magic, and it tells more about the nature of wishing and spells than any story I have ever read. At the same time, it is a wise book describing not only how these things are learnt, but when and why they should not be used in the human world.
(b)   One purchase is money well spent. Buy a good, well-bound collection of traditional Nursery Rhymes and finger plays. It will have changing uses over the next year or two. Gather him on your knee and look together at the pictures for very short periods. Let him pick out the things he knows. Read what interests him so that he hears over and over again the music of our language. He will store it in his mind and try to copy it. There will be more about the changing uses of this book in the next pamphlet.
(c)   These children were clearly getting the experience and 'feel' of the book in a way which it would be difficult to achieve by any other method. I am convinced that these skills ought to be part of the basic professional equipment of all teachers of literature and that the present system of teacher training ought to take more account of this. I am equally convinced that this teacher's effectiveness as a Drama teacher is partly based upon his skill and knowledge as a teacher of literature, also. The view that Drama should be

14

fused with English teaching in schools is one that some Drama specialists strongly oppose. I am more than ever convinced after meeting this particular teacher that drama and literature teaching are the more effective if the same teacher has responsibility for both.

(d) It was not until 1909, towards the end of an eventful though unhappy life, that Frances Hodgson Burnett began her most loved book, *The Secret Garden*. She'd just moved into her new Italianate villa at Plandome, Long Island, built with the proceeds of a very successful literary career.

The way you write will depend partly on the kind of reader you have in mind. Here is the narrator in *Under Milk Wood*, poetic and dramatic in tone.

There's the clip-clop of horses on the sun-honeyed cobbles of the sun-honeyed streets, hammering of horse shoes, gobble quack and cackle, tomtit twitter from the bird-ounced boughs, braying on Donkey Down. Bread is baking, pigs are grunting, chop goes the butcher, milk-churns bell, tills ring, sheep cough, dogs shout, saws sing. Oh, the Spring whinny and morning moo from the clog dancing farms, the bulls' gab and rabble on the boat-bobbing river and sea and the cockles bubbling in the sand, scamper of sanderlings, curlew cry, crow caw, pigeon coo, clock strike, bull bellow, and the ragged gabble of the bear-garden school as the women scratch and babble in Mrs. Organ Morgan's general shop where everything is sold: custard, buckets, henna, rat-traps, shrimp-nets, sugar, stamps, confetti, paraffin, hatchets, whistles.

Now let's look at something in a very different voice. What kind of a book might *this* passage have come from?

Though there is little to attract the hill-climber, the health-seeker, the sportsman or the week-end motorist, the contemplative may, if sufficiently attracted to spare it some leisurely hours, find, in its cobbled street and its little fishing harbour, in its several curious customs, and in the conversation of its local 'characters', some of that picturesque sense of the past so frequently lacking in towns and villages which have kept more abreast of the times. The river Dewi is said to abound in trout but is much poached. The one place of worship, with its neglected graveyard, is of no architectural interest.

It's the voice of a guidebook.

2.3
Jot down any differences you notice between the way language is used in the two extracts above. What impression is each trying to create? What does each hope to achieve?

5 Creative and Analytical Essays

I want, in the rest of this Unit, to make the very simple division between an analytical essay and a creative essay. Then I shall look at ways of collecting information for each. I call 'analytical' essays those which expect a detached treatment of the material. 'Creative' essays are ones which expect the writer either to use his own experience directly, or to make up a story – to 'invent'.

To get this distinction clear, look back at the definitions in the previous paragraph and then try the following Questions.

2.4
Say whether each of the following essay titles seems to expect (a) an **Analytical** or (b) a **Creative** approach. Write down (a) or (b) for each, along with any reservations you may have.

(i)   Compare and contrast Palmerston and Bismarck as politicians.
(ii)   A day in the life of a 2p piece.
(iii)   'When the car wouldn't start . . .'
(iv)   A critical evaluation of 'Decay'. (A poem by John Clare.)
(v)   'Society today suffers from organisations which are large and unwieldy.'
(vi)   My schooldays.
(vii)   The characteristics of land-use in the metropolitan borough of Leeds.

2.5
Here are two essay titles. First of all, make up one or two sentences of a possible opening paragraph to each of them. (If you know nothing about the causes of the First World War, don't worry – try to invent something that sounds convincing.)

Essay Title 1: Write about a time when you were afraid.
Essay Title 2: Assess the main causes of the First World War.

Have you finished? Don't read on unless you have.
Before we discuss possible answers, I would like you to have a look at another student's attempt. Here are the openings he chose:

Essay 1: Fear has meant many things at different times. Once man feared wild animals; then he feared man-made objects, like aeroplanes. In the 19th century, he feared revolution and famine . . .

Essay 2: Bodies lay pell-mell, some torn by barbed wire, some resting sadly in mud and puddles. Smoke drifted above the battlefield. No-man's land assumed an uneasy quiet . . .

Are your own openings at all similar? If not, which do you think is better, your own or that of the student quoted? Do you feel each student has interpreted correctly what the question requires? Now read the discussion.

6 The Creative Essay

Here is an example of this kind of essay. Read it, and then answer.

My First Day

It was my first day at Wisewood Secondary Modern. I was fourteen years old, alone and scared. This was my first experience of the north of England and I was hating it. On reflection, I see that I must have appeared a strange creature to my new class mates. They in their various forms of dress, from the 'flash' suit to holey jumper and holier jeans, and I in my black blazer complete with badge. All through my first lesson I saw horribly aware that I was being scrutinized by umpteen pairs of probing eyes. At break they crowded around me. 'Do you?' one of the biggest asked me. 'Do-do I what?' I replied. 'Strive to serve', he said, prodding my badge which bore the motto of my previous school. 'Sometimes', I answered, deciding to take the middle road. 'Does 'e play tennis?' shouted a wit at the back causing a few of them to laugh. When the bell rang I sighed with relief. I had come out of it unscathed although the imitations of my accent still rang in my ears.

Our next lesson was Art. I was last in and as the others sat down I went and stood in front of the master's desk. He looked up at me and glared. 'Well', he said, his teeth remaining clenched tightly together.

'I'm a new boy, sir', I murmured. He peered at me closely and grimaced as if he found me slightly distasteful.

'You're not', he retorted. 'You must be at least fourteen!' Before I could answer this unexpected reply he spoke again. 'Can you fight "newboy"?' he said aloud. The silence in the room now became absolute and once more the eyes were on me. 'Yes,' I blurted out, praying that it was the right answer. 'Good, you'll need to with this lot!', was his parting shot as he waved me to the nearest empty seat.

2.6

Read the piece again, and jot down in your notebook a sentence or two in answer to each of the following questions:

(a) What kind of essay do you feel the title expects?

(b) Do you find it an interesting essay?

(c) The essay uses some rather colloquial language. Can you find examples?

(d) Does this use of the colloquial seem to you a strength or weakness in the essay?

(e) Say whether you liked or disliked the essay.

Make sure you answer all these questions before you move on.

I hope you enjoyed looking at that essay. You will have a chance to try this kind of activity again in the first part of your Assignment for this Unit. You should now have some idea of what makes up a creative essay – liveliness, a distinctive personal voice, a good use of detail, and a relaxed relationship with the reader.

It's time for *you* to begin to write a creative essay now. First, you must collect information and the source is – yourself! In the creative essay all the material is inside you: you don't need to turn to books, though might find these stimulate you. The process is less one of *collecting* information than of *generating* it, by using memory or the imagination. We might call the process one of creative thinking – a concentrated recall. Creative writing isn't an activity reserved for 'great authors'. We are all much more creative in this way than we might think. We all gossip, tell jokes, recount our experiences, dream. In other words, we are going through the necessary processes every day, in speech rather than writing (though those of you who keep diaries or send chatty letters will also be writing in this way). Even Assignment A involved some imagining. When tackling the creative essay it is very important to write as freely as possible, and this will come with practice.

Next, you will be doing some writing on the topic 'Jottings from School'. First of all, remember the need to look closely at the question.

What kind of treatment seems to you expected by the word 'jottings'?

Surely it implies something relaxed, incomplete, even disconnected; not a full, elaborately organised piece of writing. Informality seems to be required. Here are some notes to help you further.

Look for *detail*. To do this you might ask yourself:
What happened?
Who was there?
When did it happen?
What did it look/taste/feel like?
Where did it happen?
How did it happen?
What was I wearing?
What did we eat?
i.e., ask, 'What?', 'Who?', 'When?', 'Where?', 'How?'. Remember that even ordinary things can be made vivid and interesting. Try to get into the habit of looking afresh at your surroundings.

Don't bother to put your notes into logical order. You'll do this later. Allow yourself to relax and jot them down as they come. One way to do this is to put the subject in the middle of your page and write what occurs to you as branches coming out from it. Your notes will then look something like this:

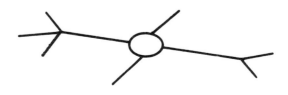

These are called 'nuclear' or 'spider' notes, and we'll come back to them later.

Now make your own jottings. You can choose your own school or a school you know well, e.g. because your brother or your friend goes there. Just jot down a collection of thoughts, feelings, events, incidents, characters – whatever you like.

Here are some of my brief 'Jottings from School':

bull

sentence rules

kept me in during an eclipse

In 'spider form' these notes look like this:

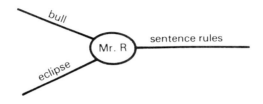

This spider plan could, of course, be added to.

Now write your notes up into a paragraph or two. Then read on. Here is my own version.

Jottings From School

Mr Randall looked like a bull – pink skin, fleshy, falling about his high white collar. He usually had a cane, which he swished about, and brought down loudly on his desk when we recited wrongly one or other of his grammar rules:

Never begin a sentence with 'and'.

A sentence is a complete thought, beginning with a capital letter and ending with a full stop.

He disliked me. I wasn't tidy in my work as he himself was – meticulous in combing down his few grey hairs, in his shiny but exact three piece suit. He kept me in once during a complete eclipse of the sun, when all the other boys were peering through bits of brown glass. How mean can you get, keeping someone in during an eclipse?

That is not a great piece of writing, but I hope it is honest and straightforward. I tried to get *involved* in the experiences I had with that teacher.

2.7
Do you think the 13-year-old who wrote the following passage was *involved* with his topic? Write a sentence or two in answer to this.

A stream trips past over rocks and gulleys carrying with it a boat made of leaves. It comes to a dam built of leaves. It rises quickly, bursts the dam and so continues on its merry way. Over stones, round banks of islands, past cows in the fields, past little children playing on the banks. The stream surges up, increasing in might . . .

7 The Analytical Essay

You should now have some idea of what a successful creative essay is like, and of how to start writing one. We move next to the second kind, the analytical essay, which I defined briefly in Section 5. Check back to page 15 to refresh your memory before I introduce a way of dealing with questions of this kind. You will be especially concerned with them if you are studying history, geography, the social sciences or the arts.

In the previous sections we looked at the problem of deciding exactly what the question wanted – remember our discussion of what 'jottings' could mean? This is even more important in the analytical essay. You have to provide exactly what the question wants, and *no more*. A question on Keats might ask you to 'Discuss his use of imagery drawn from sight, touch and smell.' A question on Bismarck might be limited to:

foreign, not domestic, policy

a particular period

a comparison with someone else.

You are not asked in either to 'Give an account of all you know . . .' The question needs the most careful scrutiny, particularly of its 'key words'.

Key Words

Most questions you answer will have words intended to guide you into writing one kind of answer rather than another. Clearly, it is important to work out the **content** of a question, but this won't be difficult – volcanoes or Bismarck, Keats or genetics. What you need to look at even more closely are the words which indicate **how** you are intended to discuss this content: the treatment you are to give.

It is not only in writing essays that we come across words which direct us. When I was at school a notice in the bus read *Do Not Spit*. Our behaviour on the words is directed all the time by signs – *No Left Turn*, *Pass Either Side*, *Give Way*, etc.

2.8
Underline the word or words which tell you how to behave, or which give you directions, in the following instructions.
Apply the paste thinly.
Plant the shoots at intervals of 3 inches.
Mix the powder with a little water.
Use blank cartridges.

2.9
1. In Section 5 of Unit 2 you were asked to look at this question: 'Assess the main causes of the First World War.' Now – underline the key word in it.

2. Underline *one* really important key word in each of the following questions. Remember, you are looking for words which tell you *how to proceed*, not for words indicating the subject (or content).
(i)   Narrate the main events of Gladstone's Second Ministry.
(ii)   Explain the principal causes of the French Revolution.
(iii)   Describe how a glacier is formed.
(iv)   Tell us what happened to you on your way to the exam room.
3. Underline the key words in the following questions, taken from an Open University exam paper. (The course is called 'Making Sense of Society'.)
(i)   Is it possible to differentiate the different social science disciplines in terms of their subject matter?
(ii)   'The study of power involves the social scientist in the analysis of patterns of social conflict.' Discuss the validity of this statement.

If you make this kind of careful analysis of your question then you are much more likely to collect material that is **relevant**. A history teacher gives two very good examples of students who have wasted their time and energy through failing to look closely enough at the question:

(a)   A question asks students to decide whether 'expediency' or 'policy' motivated reforms before 1830. Many students write an account of reforms but never use the words 'expediency' or 'policy' at all.
(b)   Another question asks 'What was the long-term significance of the chief measures of reform relating to England during Gladstone's First Ministry?' About half my students begin with reforms relating to *Ireland*. All the essays give detailed descriptions of the reforms. Not one has ever posed the question – 'What is demanded by the expression "long term significance"?' And I have marked hundreds!

At the end of this Unit there is an Appendix which will help you to work out what certain standard key words mean. You may find it useful as a source of reference in your future studies.

Collection of Material: Asking Questions

Having defined your question, you can now go on to collect material for it. You will find that the time you have spent will be well worth while. To guide your collection of material, try *asking questions*.

Can you remember where else, in this Unit, it was suggested that you might ask yourself questions in order to get ideas and material for writing?

In Section 6 (page 17), it was suggested that questions help to generate ideas and lines of enquiry for you. Even in analytical essays, it is worth getting down what you know already on a subject, and then asking questions to which you hope you will find answers from your books.*

2.10

In the light of these comments, which of the following students is carrying out a sensible policy? Why? Both are working on an essay entitled 'Give reasons for the decline of the guilds.' The course they are taking is Economic History. (Don't worry if you know nothing about the guilds or even what the study of Economic History involves. Just consider which student is proceeding most sensibly.) *You only need to write a couple of sentences.*

Student A goes to the library and gets out all the books in the History section referring to 'guilds'. He starts reading them, taking extensive notes.

Student B explores the title especially its key words. He formulates certain questions, to which he wants answers. e.g. What exactly was a 'guild'? Might they have declined through disuse, abuse or political pressure?

One thing is worth emphasising: *to ask questions of an essay title you don't need to know anything about it.* Think of every day life. An engineer repairs my central heating system, and a mechanic my car. I know nothing about either machine, but that doesn't stop me asking all sorts of questions, at least some of which will be intelligent and might get to the heart of the problem. Try this kind of question-asking in the following exercise.

2.11

The questions below are from different subjects. You probably think that you know little about most of them. Nevertheless, spend 3 or 4 minutes on each topic making up a few questions to which you would hope to find answers.

*If you want to take this idea further, read pp. 123–127 of Tony Buzan's *Use your Head*, published by the BBC. Look at his discussion of 'nuclear' notes, and 'linear' notes.

(a) Examine the problems of living in an area of volcanic activity.

(b) What steps did Gladstone take in his 'mission to pacify Ireland'?

(c) Would you agree with the statement that 'Milton used words just about as imaginatively as a bricklayer uses bricks'?

(d) What are the functions of 'attitudes' for the individual?

(e) Distinguish between the Protestant and Roman Catholic conceptions of 'God'.

(f) How do the findings of educational psychology and educational sociology help the teacher to establish order in the classroom?

The important thing to remember from your work on the last three questions is *don't just plunge into a pile of reading*. Think, and do all your preliminary work first. Ask questions to guide your study and to cut down the amount of work you have to do. (This is something you'll have been doing, too, in your earlier work on the key words of the question.) As you start your reading you will probably want to extend and refine your questions, but they will provide you with a useful framework for your reading and *thinking*.

Don't forget that there are sources other than books. There may be useful material in radio or television programmes. Casual discussions may be significant too: for these reasons it is a good idea to have a notebook handy.

Don't forget to record the sources of your ideas, e.g.

● author

● title

● publisher

● date of publication

● chapter and page number

Arranging and Storing Your Material

There are two main ways of laying out your notes: *Linear* notes and *nuclear* notes. I've already referred (in the footnote on p. 22) to Tony Buzan's discussion of these in *Use Your Head*; here is a brief explanation.

Linear notes record information in lines *across* the page. Here's an excerpt from some linear notes on 'Problems of the Railways':

A. *Problems of the Railways*
1. Finance
    (a) public service or self-financing
    (b) sources
        (i) government
        (ii) passengers
        (iii) advertising

2. Control
   (a) Parliament
   (b) changing govts have different ideas
   (c) views of individuals and bodies
   (d) passengers
   (e) private industry
   (f) the unions

3. Future Planning
   (a) commuter services
      (i) shd be run at cheaper rates?
      (ii) the profit-making part of the system?
   (b) fare policies
   (c) new rolling stock

In *nuclear* notes the main point is placed in the centre of the page, and the subsidiary points come out on stalks, or 'branches':

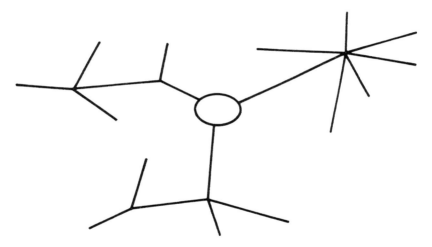

To ensure that you've grasped the idea, copy out this spider plan and add the points about the problems of the railways, already given in linear form.

You might like to practice *both* methods. You may find one method good for one stage, and the other more helpful at another stage. For example, I like to use nuclear notes to generate ideas and ask questions, but when I come to write the essay plan I find it more helpful to use the linear form.

A third method is to put your notes on *cards*, or pieces of paper, one point to each card. See the two examples below. You can buy cards of 125 mm × 75 mm or 150 mm × 100 mm. On each, you place *one* piece of information or *one* quotation, with a reference to its source. You can use one size (say 150 mm × 100 mm) for the note, and the other size for details of the reference (author, title, etc.).

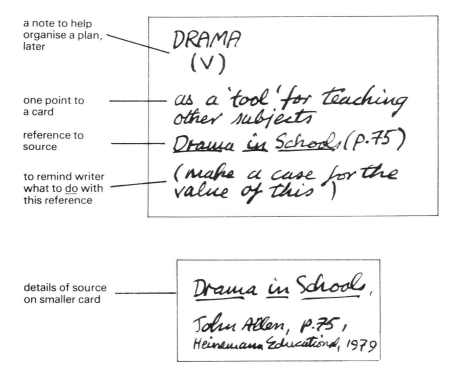

a note to help
organise a plan,
later

DRAMA
(∨)

one point to
a card

as a 'tool' for teaching
other subjects

reference to
source

Drama in Schools (p.75)

to remind writer
what to do with
this reference

(make a case for the
value of this)

details of source
on smaller card

Drama in Schools,
John Allen, p.75,
Heinemann Educational, 1979

This card system (or just paper torn to size – cheaper!) is very useful when you come to make your plan. You can take out the pieces you need, and shuffle them into the order required for writing-up.

Storage

If you choose the third method, your papers or cards can be kept in a plastic container (all good stationers have these) for as long as you need them. Or you could use an old shoe box, if expense is a problem. Nuclear and linear notes can be kept either in a good hard-backed book or in a ring file. The latter is more flexible, as papers can be taken in and out, and shuffled. It's not as flexible as the separate card idea though, as you have to put more than one point on a sheet of file paper because it's so much larger – and you'll often want to write on *both* sides of the page.

Selecting From This Material

If you have asked questions to guide your collection of material you should not have too unmanageable an amount. But even so, you will have to select and this is where you might have problems. You might feel that you want to show *how much* work you have done, i.e. to use all of it. But you must select very rigorously. In an essay of, say, 1500 words* you can make only a handful of points really fully. If you don't discard, it will be much more difficult to get these points into a clear logical sequence. You won't have wasted your time on collecting the material you don't finally use. The time you spent will have helped you to form mature views on the topic of the essay. Your grasp of that topic will be all the surer; and that, really, is the reason for doing the essay in the first place.

Some students plunge into essay writing straight after collecting their material – not a good idea. Best pause (e.g. sleep on it) and then select and discard to form your plan. This is what we shall be looking at in the next Unit.

8 Summary

These preliminary stages are an essential part of the actual writing of the essay. In this Unit we have looked at the general expectations of essays, using the analytical/creative division. Then we examined the **specific** requirements of **individual** questions, looking at key words and making careful definitions. We also looked at some ways of collecting material for each type of essay. Next we will move on to the essay plan.

9 Assignment B

There are three parts to this Assignment.
1.   You will see below a passage from a creative essay. Read it several times. Then say what you think of it. Do you like it? Can you give reasons for your opinion? (You should find the work you did for question 6, and the relevant **Discussion,** helpful for the work here). You might also like to bear in mind the following two questions:
   What sort of woman is Mrs Flower, and how does the writer reveal her character to us?

---

*To find the length of your essay don't count every single word. Your time is too valuable. Simply count the number of words in a typical line and multiply by the number of lines on the page. Then add up the number of pages and calculate the total words. Try this out when you come to Unit 4 and later Units, when you have to write essays of a certain stated length.

Does the writer have an interesting 'point of view' on the experience?

Write at least 5 or 6 sentences in your answer.

I Had Always Been . . .

I had always been rather baffled as to why my mother had anything to do with this woman – called inappropriately, Mrs Flower. I can only think that she looked after me whilst my mother worked because a lot of my childhood memories involve her and her house and family.

She was a big-boned woman with coarse features and red-veined cheeks and I considered her fascinatingly common.

Her husband died when their youngest daughter was two. I can see him in his bed, downstairs – a frail, dark-haired man who seemed very kind. She seemed to take sufficient and even sympathetic care of him in his long illness. Even I, naïve as I was, realised he was dying.

They lived in a back-to-back house, sparsely furnished but surprisingly clean. There was an old cast-iron range next to the sink and she had the habit of standing in front of this, legs astride and skirts hitched up at the back to her bum. This seemed extremely vulgar and embarrassed me considerably. Her legs were mottled shades of pink and white from sitting stockingless too close to the fire.

I always seemed to land myself in strange predicaments at this house. Once, I fell in the canal near the rec' and was led back to Mrs Flower. I had to undress and, being a very prim little girl, was in agonies whilst playing a game of mock see-saw with a young boy who kept peeking open-mouthed under the table which had seemed to be my best barrier.

2. Generate material, in the way suggested in Section 6, on *one* of the following topics:
 (i) A Frightening Experience
 (ii) A Moment of Achievement
 (iii) A Holiday I Remember Well
 (iv) Incidents from My Childhood (*at home, not at school*)

Set about this in exactly the same way as you did for 'Jottings from School', in question 6. Try to write down as many points as possible, and remember that you are trying to *interest* your reader, and trying to recapture the *detail* of the experience. Don't bother to organise these notes into a plan yet.

3. Read through the whole of this question before as starting to answer any part of it.

 Here are two analytical essay title on Education:
 (i) Explore the various motives people have for seeking to educate themselves.
 (ii) 'The education system exists to serve the needs of industry.' Evaluate this statement.

or you may carry out the following stages on an essay which you have currently been set in another subject.

Choose any *one* of the above three questions, and do the following things:

(a) Write down the title and underline *one* key word in it.

(b) Write a sentence or so on what you think the key word is directing you to do.

(c) Write down your present knowledge of, and ideas on, the subject. (Look back to pp. 22–6 for more on this process.) You can use nuclear notes, linear notes, or make notes on separate pieces of paper.

(d) Ask yourself questions about the title, in the way suggested in Section 7 of this Unit. These questions will guide you into selecting material.

(e) Note down the sources you might turn to for answers to these questions. (Books? Programmes? People? Magazines?) Try to be as specific as you can. If you have time, you could explore the topic at your library.

(f) Collect as much material as you can. Later, you'll be organising this into a plan, and then writing it up into an essay of not more than 1000 words.

Revision Exercises

Do not look at the answers at the end or look back to the Unit until you've tried all these. Write your answers down; when you have finished, look at page 29 to find the correct answers:

1. Put the following essay-writing processes in logical order:
   (a) Collection of information and material for the essay.
   (b) Making a finished copy of the essay.
   (c) Thoughtfully defining for yourself the scope of the question.
   (d) Making a rough copy of the essay.
   (e) Making an outline essay plan.
   (f) Reading over the essay carefully before giving it to your teacher.

2. Assuming you have a choice of essay topics, which is the 'odd one out' of the following, i.e. which statement is unsound?
   (a) You should choose carefully a topic which you know something about.
   (b) You should not worry too much about choosing which essay to do since they are usually all much the same as one another.
   (c) You should choose a topic which interests you, if you possibly can.
   (d) You should remember your strengths and weaknesses when choosing which essay to write in a course or in an exam.

3.   Essay titles contain 'key words' which indicate the treatment you should give them. Underline the key words in the following:
   (a)   Evaluate the success of Palmerston's foreign policy.
   (b)   Give an account of Palmerston's foreign policy.
   (c)   'Palmerston's foreign policy was fundamentally unsound'. Discuss critically.
   (d)   How did Palmerston promote British interests?
   (e)   Why did Palmerston promote British interests?

4.   Successful 'creative' essays are likely to: (*only three are right*)
   (a)   Contain material of direct interest to a reader.
   (b)   Be lively – e.g. in description, narrative or dialogue.
   (c)   Have a high percentage of very long words.
   (d)   Be written in an ornate 'literary' style.
   (e)   Use a selection of telling detail.

5.   This course cannot offer detailed advice on **every** skill that the student needs in order to write successful essays. In particular you might need further help on which *three* of the following:
   (a)   Efficient filing of material.
   (b)   Making an essay plan.
   (c)   Note taking.
   (d)   Understanding the main differences between speaking and writing.
   (e)   Reading skills.

Answers to Revision Exercises

1.   (c); (a); (e); (d); (b); (f).
2.   (b) is an unsound way of tackling essay selection. Choice is usually given so that the student can present his strengths. Not all questions will be equally easy to all students because students themselves differ – in expertise, interests, etc.
3.   (a)   'Evaluate . . .'
   (b)   'Give an account of . . .'
   (c)   'Discuss critically . . .'
   (d)   'How . . .'
   (e)   'Why . . .'
You may have underlined others as well. But these words are the major indications of the treatment expected by the question setter.
4.   (a); (b); (e)
(c) makes no sense; (d) is generally considered inappropriate now, although it may have once been valued.
5.   (a); (c); (e).
(b) and (d) are, it is hoped, adequately dealt with. All these skills are well within your grasp – especially if you have got this far in the course. Keep working: you are now well into the process of writing essays.

Appendix 1*: Some Key Words Defined

Some of the terms which are frequently used in examination questions are listed below. Make sure that you are quite clear about the precise meaning of each of them. Use this list to refer back to later in your studies.

Compare — Look for similarities and differences between; perhaps reach a conclusion about which is preferable.

Contrast — Set in opposition in order to bring out differences.

Criticise — Give your judgement about the merit of theories of opinions or about the truth of facts; back your judgement by a discussion of evidence or reasoning involved.

Define — Set down the precise meaning of a word or phrase. In some cases it may be necessary or desirable to examine different possible, or often used, definitions.

Discuss — Investigate or examine by argument; sift and debate; give reasons for and against. Also examine the implications.

Describe — Give a detailed or graphic account of.

Distinguish between *or* **Differentiate** — Look for the differences between.

Evaluate — Make an appraisal of the worth of something, in the light of its truth or usefulness.

Explain — Make plain; interpret and account for; give reasons for.

Illustrate — Make clear and explicit.

Interpret — Often means much the same as *illustrate*.

Justify — Show adequate grounds for decisions or conclusions; answer the main objections likely to be made to them.

Outline — Give the main features, or general principles, of a subject, omitting minor details and emphasising structure and arrangement.

Relate — (a) Narrate – more usual in examinations.
(b) Show how things are connected to each other, and to what extent they are alike, or affect each other.

State — Present in a brief, clear form.

Summarise — Give a concise account of the chief points of a matter, omitting details and examples.

Trace — Follow the development or history of a topic from some point of origin.

---

*This Appendix is based on a handout called *Examination Technique* from the General Studies Department at Barnet College of Further Education and compiled by A. E. Baker and V. O'Donoghue.

UNIT 3

Making the Outline Plan

1. Things to look for
2. Moving to a plan
3. Why a plan?
4. One way of planning
5. Plans must suit the essay set
6. Planning at paragraph and sentence levels
7. Assignment C
8. Revision exercises

1 Things to Look For

When you have worked through this Unit and carried out the related activities, you should be able to:

● See the relationship of this stage to the stages described in Unit 2.

● Understand the reasons for making an outline plan.

● Realise that you are planning other activities each day and that planning your essay is not so different.

● Grasp one simple way of planning, using *introduction, main body* and *conclusion*.

● Realise the possible pitfalls in writing *introductions* and *conclusions*.

● Recognise effective *introductions* and *conclusions* when you see them.

● See how planning might have to vary according to the nature of the subject.

● Understand why it is important to construct coherent sentences and paragraphs.

2 Moving to a Plan

In your work on the course so far you have guided yourself through the following stages:
(a) You have selected a question (in the light of your own strengths, weaknesses, and interests).

(b) You have thought intensively about this question:

● about the kind of treatment required.

● about the expectations of the question setter.

Here you will have examined the actual words of the question – especially any key words.
(c) You have collected material for both the creative and analytical type of essay and you have practised 'question-asking' strategies to do this effectively.

You may be feeling that writing an essay is rather an elaborate business full of 'stages' and 'processes'. But once you have worked through these and written a few essays in this way, you will soon find how effective it is. Learning *any* new set of skills is difficult at first, and you are so worried about doing it properly that you cannot relax. I went to a badminton course recently and found the learning of each stroke a complicated affair; the 'correct' arm movement seemed unnatural. But as I practised I gradually introduced the use of these correct methods into my play and the strokes became more natural.

Why a Plan?

There are three very important reasons why it is advisable to make an outline plan before writing up your essay.

● It makes a well-shaped essay much more likely.

● It makes it easier for you psychologically – you can move from point to point easily.

● It saves time. We plan in life partly because our time is limited.

Let us take the third point further. Each day brings a fresh set of jobs which we have to fit into our limited time. These get turned into a sort of list in our minds, and we then turn them into a plan – much as we need to turn our separate points and ideas into an actual outline for the essay.

One afternoon recently, I had to tackle a varied list of jobs. I had to:
shop (coffee, baby oil, biscuits, apples, a light bulb, batteries, iced
  cake, bananas, sprouts, a prescription, and plasters)
feed child
bath child
have tea myself
put casserole on for evening meal
wash up tea things
tape record a radio programme
With only limited time to do all this I had to *plan*. This is how I did it:
1. Shop (child in pushchair): Greengrocer (apples, bananas, sprouts);

Chemist (baby oil, prescription, plasters); Corner shop (biscuits, coffee, cake); Electrical shop (light bulb, batteries) in that order to form a convenient route.

2. Arrive home. Feed child and make my own tea.
3. Bath child.
4. While child in bath – put casserole on
                          – wash up tea things
                          – put on tape recorder

We don't usually put all this down on paper – it's second nature. We plan too in our speaking, both in advance and at the time.

Advance planning: We go over in our minds exactly what we are going to say to the headmaster, or to the personnel officer who is interviewing us. We run over the excuses we are going to offer our friends for forgetting to warn them that we would be late.

Planning or re-planning at the time: We adapt our plans: as we talk to the headmaster we vary our approach according to the way in which he reacts. Thus, if he is very helpful we might not want, or need, to say all that we had planned.

So we all plan, to some degree at least, every day. Since we use these planning skills in daily life, we should also be able to use them in planning our essays.

4 One Way of Planning

Look at the material you have collected and decide which point you feel is most important. You might make this your conclusion. Then sort out three or four other main points, which you will expand. Your essay would then look like this:

● Introduction

● Main body

● Conclusion

If you are given a word limit – say 1000 words – you might split it up thus:

Introduction   *125 words or less*
Main body   *600–700 words*. i.e. about 150 words or a little more for each of four points
Conclusion   *250* words or so

Doing this does help you to keep the right proportions. Also, by breaking the work into separate stages with word limits, you should find the task more manageable.

This is quite a sound plan, and reflects a logical approach. You might, for example, need to define your terms or to indicate how you intend to tackle the question. Both of these would provide appropriate material for an *introduction*. In the *main body* you could deal with three or four main points, ideas, arguments, or aspects together with illustrations and examples. In the *conclusion* you could make your final point, recall the issues raised in the introduction, indicate a possible area for further study, and review any important further implications.

Don't forget that your final plan could be in the form of linear notes, or nuclear notes (with references reminding you of the parts of books you want to refer to, or which page of your file or note book to turn to). Or, it could be in the form of a pile of cards which you have now organised into the order you are to use for writing the essay, with a point on each page and (perhaps) with special cards inserted reminding you that you are starting a new section or new paragraph.

Let us now turn to the ways in which you may *open* your essay. This is very important, as you have to make a good impression right from the start, and capture the reader's attention.

3.1
Which of the following introduction seems to you the better? The essay title is 'Account for student discontent in universities today'. *Write a sentence or two on this.*

A. The title mentions 'discontent' in 'universities', 'today', and these three words need careful scrutiny. I shall assume that 'today' means from 1960 on and that 'universities' is a term used for institutions of higher education generally. 'Discontent', too, can be the result of various factors . . .
B. Students go from home to universities at 18 and this is a time of fast change in their lives. Universities tend to be large and impersonal, yet students might come from small close-knit families. Of course, another problem is that they are used to one particular set of friends, and . . .

3.2
Study the following essay title:
    'Is *Kes* suitable for use in schools?'
What is your reaction to the student's introduction which follows?

It must be said at the outset that the writer's thoughts on this book are ambivalent, in the context of it being used as a school 'text' book.

This is particularly so, as only a short space of time has elapsed between a reading of this book and a consideration of the above mentioned proposition. That the issues and situations portrayed in the book are authentic, there can be no doubt. It is this very authenticity, which threads its way through every page, that brings us face to face with the many-sided problem, attendant to the use of this book in the school situation. Therefore we must examine with care our own reactions, and other considerations, and formulate a premise, for and against the use of *Kes*.

*A novel by Barry Hines, which has been made into a film.

34

3.3

Now underline all the bits in the extract given in question 2 which seem to you too wordy. When you've done this, take each sentence and rewrite it simply.

It is better to try to move into the essay at a high level of involvement and interest. If you are accused of long-windedness in your introductions, then make yourself move straight into a crucial point or an important definition. Don't beat about the bush!

Here is a student getting on with it right from the start of an 'O' level essay, which is entitled: 'Estimate, critically, the achievement of the Labour Government 1945–1951'. She starts:

Labour came to power prepared to carry out a definitive plan of social and economic reconstruction that was in tune with the national mood; a desire for fuller social justice and greater security.

Conclusions, too, need great care. As one tutor said: 'Conclusions should be *conclusions* and not just restatements of the argument.' Students often state a point in the introduction, expand it in the middle and then restate it at the end in a final paragraph beginning 'Thus it can be seen that . . .'. A conclusion should try to say something new, or at least make a new emphasis, or place the material in a different perspective. Here is a good conclusion of an essay at 'O' level entitled 'Describe and discuss the development of East West tensions in Europe after 1945.' The essay ends:

The Berlin crisis alerted the West to the threat of Russian aggression, and led to the formulation of NATO, a formidable power block including the USA. The West could only produce three million men as against four million in the Soviet Union. However, the USA had the atom bomb. Mutual assistance treaties were made by Russia with other Eastern states; but the West was determined to arrest further extensions of communism in Europe, by force if necessary. East and West were irreconcilable.

5 Plans Must Suit the Essay Set

It is important to remember that different questions require different kinds of organisation. A question asking you to 'narrate' would expect a step-by-step sequence of events or incidents, whereas a question asking for a 'contrast' would look for the drawing of clear distinctions between issues, people, or events.

The creative essay is often looser in structure than the analytical. It gives you more freedom, and you can allow the experience to take what shape it needs.

Some science and social science essays, on the other hand, expect something like the following highly organised structure:

Section 1.   Summary of previous work and research in the field. Definition of relevant terms.
Section 2.   An account of the experimental procedure used.
Section 3.   Results.
Section 4.   Discussion of the results, and any indications as to further work needed.

Your subject teacher will help you find the appropriate structure, but generally, it is fair to say that the shape of an essay will be the result of:

● The reader it's written for (see Unit 2, Section 4)

● The nature of the subject (see Unit 2, Section 3)

● The aim (i.e. as indicated by the *key words* – remember Section 7 of Unit 2).

6 Planning at Paragraph and Sentence Levels

We have talked above about essay planning. It is as well to remember that planning should take place at 3 levels.

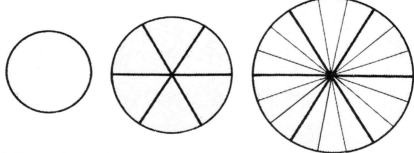

1. The essay is planned *as a whole:* the paragraphs together form *one coherent statement* which is the essay.

2. Each paragraph is planned – i.e. the sentences within them form a coherent whole.

3. Each sentence is planned – i.e. satisfying and complete in itself.

It is very important for ideas *within the essay* to 'add up' to an overall statement, and for each of the *paragraphs* to have a unity. Paragraphs should also be linked together in as natural a way as possible. Each *sentence* should be clear and accurate. This is all part of the craft of writing, something we shall return to in the next Unit. I don't suggest you should or could plan *all* this in advance. But you should plan the essay outline beforehand and remain aware of the other levels while writing it up. If you are very weak at connecting paragraphs, though, you might want to do some planning at this level as well. The exercises that follow are intended to help you to think about these problems of organisation at the levels of the sentence and paragraph.

3.4
The sentences in the paragraph below have been mixed up. 'Unmix' them to form the order that seems to you to make the most sense.

Ask him to remove any circulars or anything else that might advertise your absence. Tell the police when you are going away and also whether your neighbour has the spare key. Of course your neighbour would expect you to do the same for him! You might even get him to cut your grass – yet another give away for the thief. If you are going on holiday ask a neighbour to keep an eye on the house and report anything suspicious to the police.

3.5
The following is a letter from the Archbishop of Canterbury and others to *The Times* of 10th December 1975. All paragraphing has been left out. Can you identify the original six paragraphs? Try to underline the first sentence of each paragraph (the first one is easy of course!) Your work on this will help you with Assignment C, so its worth spending time on this and getting to know the passage.

Sir, In the face of increasing violence and politically motivated killing, we share the deep anguish of all the victims and the anger of our fellow citizens. We condemn terrorism, however motivated, without qualification. It cannot lead to greater justice or to a more compassionate society. It is totally incompatible with the Christian faith. In the light of that, we understand the motives and feelings of those who call for the reintroduction of capital punishment. However, for reasons that owe nothing to sentimentality, we believe that this would be a tragic mistake. Indeed it would be a victory for the terrorists. For the state to bring back executions and so return to a relic of a bygone age, would be to concede that Britain feels itself forced to resort to methods of law enforcement commonly used in a political context by nations whose methods we properly condemn as tyrannical. There is not the slightest guarantee that by killing the killers the level of social violence would be decreased. The opposite is at least as likely. The creation of martyrs, as Anglo-Irish history has shown in the past, is not the best road to peace. The hanging of terrorists would add one more macabre and violent element to the present situation. In Ireland it might well bring civil war closer. For us as Christians there is a more fundamental argument still. There is an ultimate sense in which judgement must be left to God. Our officers of law fulfil a function in our national life which is indispensable for its health and wellbeing, but there comes a point – when life and death itself are at stake – where weak and fallible humans must say: this is where we give place to divine judgement and mercy. 'Vengeance is mine, says the Lord: I will repay.' It would be wrong to place on any of our fellow citizens, not least on a Home Secretary who would have to advise the Crown, the appalling responsibility of deciding whether a convicted person should live or die. If this is true in a strictly criminal context, it is doubly true when crime is politically motivated. It is the awesome task of our rulers to protect all our citizens. It is for us as Christians to help them fulfil that task. It will, we believe, be made harder if the state, in our name, adds to the number who die. Our will to build a compassionate society leads us to the conviction that justice is not best served by retribution. The sanctity of human life is indivisible. At a time when reverence for life is at risk in many other contexts, both at home and abroad, our nation, if it abides by that principle even under severe provocation, will contribute significantly to a more sane and humane world.

Yours faithfully,

Turn to page 39 to see how the letter was originally divided up. Compare it with your own. Don't worry if yours is different – the object was to get you to think about paragraphs. If the Archbishop paragraphed differently, see if yours is a better division! If you are uncertain, discuss it with your teacher.

3.6
This is quite an ambitious exercise taken from the Open University's A100 Arts Foundation Course; but it's very useful.

You have been engaged for several weeks researching among the private papers and possessions of a British politician named Jones (please note that Jones is a completely imaginary character, invented for the purpose of this exercise). You have discovered:

1. A letter dated 9th December 1909 from the then Prime Minister to Jones referring to the recently passed Labour Exchanges Act, and saying: 'although the world has not yet had the chance to appreciate your invaluable labour, I shall always remember that you, my dear Jones, were the true progenitor of the Act'.

2. Certain household accounts showing that over a fifteen-year period Jones consumed ten bottles of brandy a week.

3. Various newspaper cuttings and letters from party leaders dating from the 1906 election showing that Jones was definitely regarded then as a rising politician.

4. Jones's marriage certificate 3rd May 1903.

5. A transcript of the court proceedings in which his wife successfully divorced him, March 1911.

From standard parliamentary sources you know that Jones never achieved office, and that in fact he faded out of politics during the First World War. From the parish register in his home village you find his date of birth as 20th August 1873.

In your notebook, *communicate* this information in the form of a brief piece of continuous writing. When you have finished your work, look carefully at the specimen answers and **Discussion**.

7 Assignment C

1. Turn back to the notes you made in Assignment B, part 2 (Unit 2, page 27). Make a plan for this topic and write an essay of about 500 words.
2. Refer back to the material you collected for question 4 (Assignment B). Now organise this into a simple plan. (You needn't fit all your material into the essay when you write it up later as an Assignment.)

I suggested earlier in this Unit that you select three or four main points or aspects. Don't forget that it helps to have *examples* to illustrate them.
3. Below you will find two documents on capital punishment. A copy of the letter from the Archbishop of Canterbury and others to *The Times*, which you have already worked on, and an Editorial from *The Times* (10.12.75). These are your sources for the following question:

Neither the Archbishop nor *The Times* feels that it would be right to re-introduce the death penalty, but they reach this conclusion for different reasons. Summarise the argument of each, bringing out as clearly as you can this difference. Then outline your own views on the subject. Make sure that you support your views in a reasoned way.

For this assignment you should:
(a) Analyse the question – e.g. underline the key words; make some comments on what it seems to require.
(b) Ask yourself questions about the essay title (N.B. you might use nuclear notes to help you to do this).
(c) Read the articles to extract the relevant material. This is your note-taking stage. Remember the advice given earlier and the three possible ways of taking notes – linear, nuclear, notes on separate pieces of paper.
(d) Make your plan, as a framework for writing up the essay (which you'll do as part of Assignment D).

It might help if you allow a gap between the four parts of this Assignment, especially between parts (c) and (d) – to allow time for you to assimilate the material. Allow plenty of time for this question as it is not an easy one. It should test your understanding of Units 2 and 3.

Archbishop's Letter
Sir, In the face of increasing violence and politically motivated killing, we share the deep anguish of all the victims and the anger of our fellow citizens. We condemn terrorism, however motivated, without qualification. It cannot lead to greater justice or to a more compassionate society. It is totally incompatible with the Christian faith.

In the light of that, we understand the motives and feelings of those who call for the reintroduction of capital punishment. However, for reasons that owe nothing to sentimentality, we believe that this would be a tragic mistake.

Indeed it would be a victory for the terrorists. For the state to bring back executions and so return to a relic of a bygone age, would be to concede that Britain feels itself forced to resort to methods of law enforcement commonly used in a political context by nations whose methods we properly condemn as tyrannical.

There is not the slightest guarantee that by killing the killers the level of social violence would be decreased. The opposite is at least as likely. The creation of martyrs, as Anglo-Irish history has shown in the past, is not the best road to peace. The hanging of terrorists would add one more macabre and violent element to the present situation. In Ireland it might well bring civil war closer.

For us as Christians there is a more fundamental argument still. There is an ultimate sense in which judgement must be left to God. Our officers of law fulfil a function in our national life which is indispensable for its health and wellbeing, but there comes a point – when life and death itself are at stake – where weak and fallible humans must say: this is where we give place to divine judgement and mercy. 'Vengeance is mine, says the Lord: I will repay.'

It would be wrong to place on any of our fellow citizens, not least on a Home Secretary who would have to advise the Crown, the appalling responsibility of deciding whether a convicted person should live or die. If this is true in a strictly criminal context, it is doubly true when crime is politically motivated.

It is the awesome task of our rulers to protect all our citizens. It is for us as Christians to help them fulfil that task. It will, we believe, be made harder if the state, in our name, adds to the numer who die. Our will to build a compassionate society leads us to the conviction that justice is not best served by retribution. The sanctity of human life is indivisible. At a time when reverence for life is at risk in many other contexts, both at home and abroad, our nation, if it abides by that principle even under severe provocation, will contribute significantly to a more sane and humane world.

Yours faithfully,

Times Editorial 10.12.75

Would the Death Penalty Help?

Tomorrow the House of Commons is again considering the question of capital punishment for terrorism. The question naturally divides into two parts. Is capital punishment for terrorism morally justified, and if it is morally justified, is it expedient? About the first part of the question we have no doubt: the situation which the terrorists have created is one of war. They do not hesitate to kill innocent British citizens in large numbers in Northern Ireland, and in smaller numbers elsewhere in the United Kingdom.

The morality of killing the terrorists cannot properly be distinguished from the morality of killing enemy soldiers in war. It is true that terrorists usually have to be arrested and tried, whereas enemy soldiers are killed in battle. But that is a variation of form and not of substance. Terrorists operate in a secret way and take lives by secret means. In conventional war secret agents are liable to execution when detected, and in this sense terrorists are secret agents.

We believe, therefore, that the morality of capital punishment in terrorist cases is at one with the morality of killing enemy soldiers in the conduct of justifiable and defensive war. There are, of course, pacifists who, for Christian or other reasons, regard any taking of life by the state as wrong. That has never been the view of this newspaper and we do not take it in this case.

The question, therefore, is one of advantage. Granted that we are entitled to take the lives of terrorist murderers: is it in fact helpful to the cause in which we are fighting them to do so? Here there are a number of subsidiary arguments. It is clear that capital punishment for terrorists would lead to further terrorist outrages of one sort or another. The terrorists could be expected to apply the doctrine of a life for a life and more innocent people would be killed. If it were necessary for the successful prosecution of the anti-terrorist campaign to accept that risk, then it could well be right to accept these casualties. In a war one does not hesitate to hit the enemy because the enemy might hit back. But obviously if it cannot be shown that capital punishment will help in the main campaign these consequential casualties are merely a waste of lives.

There are also difficulties of a technical character about the drafting of a Statute which defines terrorism. These difficulties would not seem to be insuperable. All legal systems divide criminal homicide into different categories, even if only into the categories of murder and manslaughter. We would not doubt the ability of a jury to determine whether a particular murder was done for terrorist reasons or not. Again, if the balance of advantage lay in the restoration of capital punishment for terrorist murders, the technical problems would not be an insuperable barrier.

It is also probable, though by its nature hard to prove, that some terrorists would be deterred by capital punishment. Certainly terrorists assume that death is a real deterrent. The precise weight to be given to the deterrent argument is not easy to assess, but it must be given some.

The question, however, comes down to a more central matter of judgment: how best can we overcome the IRA? How best can we deal with any other terrorist groups that may operate in Britain? At present the right course would seem to be to try and isolate them from support. The IRA have virtually no support outside the Irish Roman Catholic communities of Southern and Northern Ireland, the United States and Britain. They sometimes have a little technical support from other terrorist organizations or paymasters, but the community on which they wholly depend is Irish and Catholic.

The objective of policy is therefore to isolate the IRA from the Irish Roman Catholic community. At the present moment this policy has had considerable success. The great majority of Irish Catholics now distrust and fear the IRA; many hate them. Their most recent outrages in Ulster and in Britain have placed them in almost total moral isolation.

The Government of the Republic of Ireland have gone further in seeking to suppress IRA activities than at any previous stage in the emergency. They have fought a by-election in a marginal seat on the issue of security and they won it very handsomely. There are undoubtedly further steps which could be taken. In particular it is frustrating that a man who commits a murder in England cannot be extradited from Southern Ireland if he pleads that the murder was undertaken for political reasons. Nevertheless, when the emergency began, Southern Ireland could be regarded as a secure base for the IRA and now it is very far from that.

Isolated

The latest reports, even from Protestant sources, tell us that the same process has gone a long way in Northern Ireland, and that the IRA there are now largely isolated from the rest of the Catholic community. They are coming to be regarded as killers who have no concern for their own people, as a source of danger and not of defence. The same is again unquestionably true of the relationship between the IRA and the great mass of the Irish community in England. It is true, further, of the relationship between the IRA and the priests and authorities of the Roman Catholic Church. The Roman Catholic Church has of course condemned terrorist methods, but the attitude is now more profoundly indignant at this evil.

If the long campaign to restore peace to Northern Ireland is to be won, then this isolation of the IRA from its community and from its potential support has to be taken further and completed. One only has to ask whether executions would or would not tend to isolate the IRA still further from their Irish Catholic communities to see that they could not do good. Therefore, it would be contrary to the major strategy of defeating the IRA to reintroduce capital punishment.

That must be the conclusion. Capital punishment for terrorist offences is both morally permissible, and feasible, though it would cause casualties on our side, but it would be strategically damaging. It would give the IRA an advantage which it is not in our interests to give them. They would lose a comparatively small number of active men who, having been caught, would in any case be subject to long-term imprisonment but they would gain support that they could not otherwise gain. That is why most senior policemen and most senior Army officers and civil officials in Northern Ireland, and most senior policemen and the judges in England do not want capital punishment for these terrorists. Those who command the fight against the IRA believe that it would make the fight more difficult for them.

Great strain

It does not follow that this would always be so. It is possible that at some stage the strategy of detaching the IRA from its base of support might be seen to have failed, and that the alternative strategy which is one of total repression of the IRA regardless of the effect of the methods on their potential supporters, might be followed. But this strategy itself has great and obvious dangers and disadvantages. No government so far has been prepared to follow it, and so long as there is any prospect of ultimate success for the strategy of alienating the Catholic community from the IRA, it is right to continue to apply it. There is at present more than hope, there is solid evidence that the IRA is losing ground in its own community.

At the same time the political policy which has been pursued so far does impose great strain on the community in Northern Ireland and a strain on the community in the rest of the United Kingdom. It needs to be reinforced by a very tough determination to overcome the IRA by existing methods. In particular so far as Northern Ireland is concerned the Army must be given freedom to conduct the most efficient military operations against the IRA.

42

The situation in south Armagh does not suggest that they have all the support they need. In Britain additional resources may need to be given to the police; it may even be necessary to consider the question of police pay outside the general strategy of incomes policy in order to bring police manpower up to desirable levels. Recent successes only emphasize the fact that these men have to be caught. The ability to catch them is more important than the punishment after they have been convicted. It would certainly be wrong to punish those we catch in such a way as to win support for their movement.

Reproduced from The Times with permission.

Your written answers to these three parts form Assignment C. When you get this work back study your teacher's comments carefully.

8 Revision Exercises

Again, try all these *before* you look at the answers, or back at the Unit. Write down your responses in your notebook. Then correct your own work.

1. Which of the following statements is the 'odd one out'? i.e. with which one would the author of this Unit disagree?
   (a) Your work on the essay starts when you begin to think about it.
   (b) Essay writing is divided into stages which are quite separate from one another.
   (c) It is important to be an organised student.
   (d) The learner should remain active throughout.

2. 'When confronted with an unfamiliar subject, it is possible to ask questions about it.' Would the author of this Unit:
   (a) agree *or* (b) disagree?
   Say why in one sentence.

3. Which of the following is incorrect?
   Good essay questions:
   (a) Seek to find out what your strengths are rather than your weaknesses.
   (b) Are carefully phrased so that you can answer them in the word limit suggested.
   (c) Are set to trick you if possible.
   (d) Presuppose some general skills of thinking and use of language.

4. If you feel you need to acquire more general skills of systematic study you should: (*three are correct*)
   (a) Give it up, as it is useless.
   (b) Take a yoga course.

(c) Go to a psychoanalyst.
(d) Take an evening course on 'Systematic Study' at a local college.
(e) Read some of the relevant books in the booklist at the end of this course.

Answers to Revision Questions

1. (b) is the 'odd one out'. All the time, I try to stress the interdependence of the stages, which are broken up and looked at separately only for convenience.

2. (a) Agree. I have suggested that questions can be asked irrespective of subject matter or learner's knowledge.

3. (c) I hope you noticed the key word 'good' in the question. Unfortunately, essay setters sometimes fall down! Even when they do, you will usually get credit since the marker will be aware of the unnecessary difficulty of the question.

4. (d) and (e) are correct – though enthusiasts for yoga and psychoanalysis might argue for (b) and (c) too!

UNIT 4

Practical Matters: Presentation

1. Things to look for
2. Moving from outline to essay
3. Clear expression:
   clear thinking leads to clear expression preserving a clear
   structure: paragraphing 'correctness' and 'grammar'
   common errors in English
4. Use of quotations in Essays:
   two types of source
   why we need quotations
   quotations need interpreting
5. How to present the essay:
   its appearance on the page
   handwriting
   references
   abbreviations
6. A note on the requirements of analytical writing
7. Assignment D
8. Revision exercises

1 Things to Look For

After working through this Unit, and carrying out the related
activities, you should be able to plan the layout and organise the clear
presentation of your essays. In particular you should be able to:

● See how the earlier stages relate to this one.

● Decide whether or not it would help you to write a rough essay
  before the finished version.

● Realise the dangers of clumsy and badly thought out sentences.

● Recognise the need for a clear structure in your final essay.

● Spot some of the more common errors in the writing of English.

● Be aware of the value of careful punctuation.

● Recognise some of the pitfalls of using quotations.

● List your sources clearly.

● Recognise and use some common abbreviations.

2 Moving From Outline to Essay

How the Earlier Stages Help You With This One

The previous Unit took you through the stage of constructing an essay outline. You have now to write this up into the essay proper. It is important to remind yourself that most of the work is now done! If you have carried out the earlier stages thoroughly and thoughtfully, you'll have gone through the most difficult part. Writing up the essay is a demanding stage but it shouldn't take very long compared to the earlier steps. You will have material you have mastered and points which are essential to your answer in the form of a clear outline. You now have to turn this into a piece of lucid continuous prose. From now on your attention should be firmly on the job of communicating with your distant reader.

Should You Pause Between Outline and Essay?

4.1
Many teachers would advise you to pause between forming your plan and writing up the essay. Why do you feel they would offer this advice?

Two Versions of the Essay?

Some teachers would say that you can move straight from your outline into the finished product. Others, that you should write out a rought copy, leave it a day, and then write out a polished version.

4.2
What do you think are the advantages and disadvantages of writing two versions of the essay, that is, a rough copy first and then a final copy?

3 Clear Expression

Clear Thinking Leads to Clear Expression

If your thoughts are clear and organised, there is very much more likelihood that your style will be too. Muddled writing is very often the result of muddled thinking, not only during your writing, but much more importantly, during your preparatory work.

4.3

Put yourself in the position of a teacher marking the following pasage from an essay on D. H. Lawrence's *Sons and Lovers* and answer these two questions in your notebook: (a) What is wrong with the passage? (b) Try to rephrase it to make its point more clearly.

Paul Morel and the author, being the same person, quite clearly had the intelligence to extract goodness from their father, whose working class was preferred to the wife's middle-class, by means of cajoling and talking and understanding, and so bring to the surface the father's introspection, so noticeably missing from the pages and the life.

The total avoidance of introspection of Morel in the book highlights what the man may have had in his mind, and serves to point the finger of guilt of bias on the author.

Preserving a Clear Structure: Paragraphing

Your outline will probably be in a form that can be turned easily into a structure of paragraphs. Remember the importance of having a clear structure: your outline should help you to achieve this. Each paragraph should have at least one main idea, and the best place for this is often the first sentence. (For more on paragraphing, refer back to Unit 3.)

'Correctness' and 'Grammar'

Many students are very worried about their inability to write 'proper English'. It would need a whole course to discuss the English language and the way it works. It would need yet another course to go into the principles of spelling and punctuation. If you are worried about these, you might find *A New English Course* by Rhodri Jones (Heinemann Educational), helpful. A good dictionary is essential, and you may also wish to refer to one of the standard works mentioned in Section 3 of the Bibliography at the end of the course. (N.B. It is better to refer to these books when you have a *specific problem* – don't try to read them all through.)

But remember that you may become inhibited if you are constantly aware of a pile of 'how to write English' manuals on the table where you work. Here is some sensible advice given to one set of students:

Mechanical Accuracy
Spelling, grammar and punctuation are important – but do not sacrifice fluency by worrying about them. Always check your essay over for spelling mistakes, particularly those of the 'there/their' nature; for errors in grammar, such as beginning a sentence in one tense and ending it in another (unintentionally); and for mistakes in punctuation such as omitting inverted commas for speech, or forgetting question marks or apostrophes. Above all,

never think 'I was hopeless at grammar and spelling at school, so I cannot write essays'. This is *not* true of most people.

You need to develop an awareness of your own strengths and weaknesses in the matter of mechanical accuracy. Here is where you need to take very careful note of what your teacher says, and of corrections on your work. *Understand* where you are going wrong and put the points right. If you keep repeating the same error and can't see why, discuss it with your teacher and maybe that's the time to consult one of the books I mentioned above.

Always read your final essay aloud before sending it off, to see if you can spot errors, inaccuracies or unclear expressions. This can't be emphasised enough. Students often lose marks or go down a grade just because they can't be bothered, or haven't left time, to carry out this final crucial check. And you might get a friend to read it through too, though always consider his suggestions carefully and critically. He'll be valuable as someone reading the essay for the first time – but he may not always be right.

Common Errors in English

No one will complain as long as you succeed in making your meaning clear. Teachers vary in their attention to formal written expression (which, incidentally, is governed not by 'rules' but by custom). But you may be particularly concerned about your ability to spot specific inaccuracies in using language, so try the following.

Here are some confusions or mistakes selected from a small file of scripts. Can you put them right?

(a) Spell these words correctly:

revultion	consistant
exsposure	dissapointed
accomodate	recieved
definate	freindship
reccomend	

(b) Show the correct use of each word in a separate sentence:
who's; whose
it's; its
perpetrated; perpetuated
principal; principle
practice; practise
they're; there; their

Check these out for yourself by reference to any good dictionary and a good punctuation guide. Your dictionary is your most valid language stand-by, but if you are still doubtful ask your teacher.

I wouldn't want you to get this section out of proportion. General matters of organisation and expression are much more important than details of spelling and punctuation. But generally a weakness in such details does unfortunately go with other more significant weaknesses. See the next section.

4.4
Here is an exercise on (a) paragraphing and (b) punctuation. Read it through and then decide how you would punctuate it and where you would put the paragraphs. (I suggest 3 paragraphs.) Indicate your paragraphs without copying out the whole passage.

of course in an actual course you will be able to go farther since you will realise what kind of question your discipline asks eg if (v) were in a course on Religious Education you would be alert to the concepts used and the appropriate discourse so dont just
5   plunge into a pile of reading ask questions to guide your study (and to cut it down) as you read you will want to extend and refine your questions and maybe cross some of your marginal ones out do not be afraid to use other sources than books there may be useful material in Radio or TV programmes (eg a radio
10 debate between Protestants and Catholics a TV documentary about a volcanic area) casual discussions may be significant too for these reasons it is a good idea to carry a notebook with you wherever you go and dont forget to record the sources of your ideas as we shall see it is important to attribute the sources of any quotations and may use in your essay record
author
title
publisher
date of publication

We use punctuation to indicate to the reader how he is to read the words, how the words are grouped, how their meaning is arranged. In speaking we use other ways of doing this, e.g. pauses, silence, gesture. Punctuation is something we have to develop as a substitute for all these other methods. (You might add this to our list of differences given in the **Discussion** of question 1.6. In speaking we have to pronounce words accurately but we don't have to punctuate. In writing we are very much concerned with punctuation but not at all with pronunciation!)

4.5
Here is the first third of a student's essay. Imagine that you are a teacher. What comments and corrections would you make? (You can use the margin of your text as if it were the actual margin on the student's essay.)

It is natural for D. H. Lawrence to include in his writings, life in mining communities, after all he was the son of a miner. 'Sons and Lovers' is not only a novel, about a man coming to terms with himself and the people he comes into contact with, but a story of community life in the late nineteenth century and the early twentieth.

There is an early mention in the first chapter of how mining communities came together, the closing down of the small 'gin pits' and centralisation by big mining companies, building larger mines. It was this centralisation, which gave the mining village its own particular way of life. The large companies built houses for the miners, 'The Bottoms' were this type of housing, The Bottoms consisted of six blocks of miners dwellings two rows of three, like the dots, on a blank six domino. It is here where can be seen the true ethos of mining community life, a lifestyle governed by various factors. The closeness of the houses brought people together, they shared each others joys and miseries, they helped each other, they knew each others business.

A tipe of narrow black alleys with ash pits, low walls, women chatting over the back wall, children playing in the backs, and around the front a different world. The fronts of the houses only reflected a neat tidy existence, neat lawns and gardens, neat parlours hardly ever used, a place to go when dressed in ones 'Sunday best'. At the turn of the century this was not every Sunday.

The closeness of the housing helped make a close community, but the one thing, which drew them together the most, was the menfolk, all were miners, they all knew each others jobs, it was this particular hazardous job, that made the miners true comrades, and put each man working below ground on equal terms. In times of trouble each man would join together and become a team in a rescue attempt or in sickness, when Morel was ill his workmates helped with a little cash just to make sure his family would not starve.

4 Use of Quotations in Essays

Two Types of Source

Students often fail to use quotations in the most telling way. Such quotations may be from two main sources:

● Primary

● Secondary

Primary sources are 'the originals', *secondary* sources are books and articles written *about* the originals. Milton's *Paradise Lost* is a primary source; Waldock's critical views on *Paradise Lost* are a secondary source. Primary sources may be of various kinds, for example: a picture by Michelangelo; the remains of an 18th century water mill; an original Beethoven manuscript; a cathedral.

A lot will depend on the purpose, topic and level of study – but this basic division should be satisfactory for your needs.

Why We Need Quotations

Quotations can be useful in various ways:
(a)   Literature students will need to refer to their primary source, e.g.

a novel or poem, to illustrate their own ideas.

(b) A history student will want to refer to the actual words spoken or written by a Prime Minister or other statesman.

(c) A sociology student will want to use contrasting definitions of a key term, before moving on to his own version.

Quote to Serve Your Own Purposes

But notice how, in the examples above, the quotations are *serving the student's own purposes*. Too often the inclusion of quotations obstructs the student's own voice. Sometimes students even quote points they don't really understand, but feel to be in some way significant. Never quote material you aren't sure of.

Don't let quotations run away with you. If possible, refer your reader to a page or passage, if you know he has the same book as you. Try to weave your quotations into your own argument. Often the use of quite brief phrases, or even single words, can show how thoroughly you have made the text your own: in such cases, the use of quotations is natural, relaxed, almost casual (like the way we recall phrases used by people we know well, when we report what they have said).

4.6
Here is an example of a student writing about *Lord of the Flies*. She is not using quotations but something very close to them: detailed reference to the text. Can you pick out the two *detailed* references she makes which both show her knowledge of the book, and also illustrate her analysis of Jack's character?

Jack . . . already shows a hint of suppressed violence in his nature, when one recalls his angry blue eyes and a habit of driving his sheath knife into tree trunks.

You should have picked out 'angry blue eyes' and the 'habit of driving his sheath knife into tree trunks' as detailed references. These show the reader that the student is familiar with the details of the book, and that she can illustrate her analysis of Jack's character; the details show his 'suppressed violence'.

4.7
Read the following essay. Underline the quotations; comment on their length and how they are used. Then answer this question: do you fell the structure of the essay is satisfying? *Write a few sentences on these points.*

Note: Many of you will not have read *Bleak House* and may find the following information useful in understanding the essay:

Mr Smallweed is a small-time speculator;

Doodle, Boodle and Foodle are incompetent administrators;
Chesney Wold is the Dedlock estate;
Tom-All-Alones is a slum district in London;
Jo is a slum dweller;
Volumnia and the Honourable Bob Sharples are aristocratic hangers-on;
Vholes is a rather nasty character.

Consider Dickens' treatment of money and property in 'Bleak House'

1   The Smallweed family is Dickens' clear picture of a family based on money grubbing, trickery and exploitation. Mr Bucket testifies that anyone of the family would 'sell the other for a quid or two'. When Chick explains to his grandfather about Guppy's generosity, the
5   venerable sage tells him to milk his friend dry and 'learn by his foolish example'. 'I'll lime you, I'll lime you', is Mr Smallweed's amiable cry before he lapses into the pleasing speculation which his education has prepared him for.

    The Dedlock family is Dickens' picture of a family based on property.
10   Sir Leicester is decent enough but hopelessly imprisoned within the walls of his own castle. He shudders at every move in the Wat Tyler direction, not so much out of any personal selfishness as a genuine feeling that England cannot survive without Doodle and Boodle. 'There is much good in the fashionable world . . . it has its appointed place'
15   but its greatest crime is that it is totally ignorant of the other worlds around it. In its own way Chesney Wold houses as much filth as Tom-All-Alones. Instead of Jo's real parasites, Sir Leicester has Volumnia and the Honourable Bob Sharples, 'that something left over which nobody knows what to do with'. But this is not a real connection
20   between Chesney Wold and Tom-All-Alones, between Lady Dedlock and Jo. How can there be any connection between them when Snagsby who lives close by is shocked by the unfamiliar world of Tom-All-Alones? But there is a connection all the same and it is one of diseases for the pestilence spreads out from Tom-All-Alones as surely as it does
25   from Chancery, with disease, taunts, sneers and theft. 'Tom has his revenge.' 'To be hustled, and jostled and moved on' is the central experience of all the characters and this is as true for Lady Dedlock as it is for Jo. The plot with its quick geographical shifts from Chesney Wold to the squalor of London forces the two together. It forces us to
30   compare the Honourable Bob Sharples and Volumnia with the brick-makers and their wives, it forces us to look at the Honourable Bob's and Volumnia's intentions to secure pensions with no responsibility attached at the same time as we realise 'what the poor are to the poor is little known except to themselves and God.' The society based on
35   exploitation is shown up for what it is, more poison comes from Tom-All-Alones than all the Boodles and Foodles can 'cure in five hundred years – though born expressly to do it'.

    'In all honesty', says Vholes ('and honesty is my golden rule whether I lose by it or gain and I generally find that I lose') the problem is 'in one
40   word, money'. Vholes exploits Richard Carstone by his respectability. He is in private life a good son and an excellent father; in public life he watches his prey as attentively as his official cat watches the mousehole

in the wall. Skimpole is equally engaged in exploiting Richard; money and the acquisition of money exposes the true character of the society.

45 Bucket tells Esther that as soon as a man says he knows nothing about money she had best look after her own. Therefore, Dickens makes a simple attack on selfishness through his treatment of money, but he also shows how the society does not understand money. Snagsby gives Jo half a crown when he is hopeless; he thinks it is 'a magic balsam for

50 all evils'. Even though Snagsby is far kinder than a Skimpole, he represents a guilty reaction, an attempt to smother and hide something, and he chooses to do it with the obvious product of this misery, his money. For Snagsby's money no less than Sir Leicester Dedlock's is based on the oppression of people like Jo. The society is frightened; the

55 policeman's hypothesis that 'every one is either robbing or being robbed' is correct.

The property based on this money is equally unsound. The property of each individual reflects that individual's character but it reflects something else, it reflects the hell of Tom-All-Alones. Until Tom-All-

60 Alones is destroyed, the world of Chesney Wold can never be real, for just as the good Vholes and the bad Vholes is a vision of terror, so is the dignity of Chesney Wold and the horror of Tom-All-Alones.

Quotations Need Interpreting

Not only should you never copy uncritically what someone else has said: you should always be prepared to *interpret* your quotations. Never leave them like isolated boulders. Work them into the structure of your essay; and the longer the quotation the more you'll have to do to integrate it.

Once again you'll be much more likely to carry out all these processes if you've worked thoroughly on the earlier stages – e.g. assimilating the reading you have carried out. Much better to have got the ideas thoroughly clear yourself, and to express them in a way unique to you, than to 'lift' somebody else's words. This understanding takes time, but iis well worth it in the increased grasp of the subject you will have.

5 How to Present the Essay

Its Appearance on the Page

Your final essay should, at the very least, be clear, tidy and legible. Don't spend too long on the presentation, but is important to observe certain aspects of lay-out:

● Leave a generous margin on the left hand side of the page, for your teacher's comments.

● Leave a space for comments at the bottom of the page.

- If you type (and it does help!) then use double-spacing (and type on one side of the paper only).

- It may be useful to keep a carbon copy of your essay – in case the original gets lost.

- Some essay questions include clear and specific advice on lay-out. They may ask you to tackle the question under certain headings (e.g. [I] A Survey of the Research, [II] The Problem Defined, [III] The Experiment . . . etc.) You should, of course, follow any such instructions meticulously.

Handwriting

Some of us have difficulty with this; there is an example of my own handwriting below. You'll see it's far from ideal.

If you write your essays by hand and *your* writing is hard to read, then try the following activity (taken from Maddox, *How to Study*, Pan Books):
(a)   Give a specimen of your handwriting to a couple of friends. Ask them to underline any letters, or combinations of letters, which they find difficult to read.
(b)   Get your friends to tell you what it is about these underlined sections that causes difficulty. e.g. words crowded; words joined; loops from one line getting tangled up with those of lines above or below.
(c)   Analyse your problems in the light of (a) and (b) and try to put things right.

References

You should carefully acknowledge any ideas you have borrowed from other sources. Clearly you cannot do this for *every* idea, but you certainly should for the main ones. Never lift sentences from books without acknowledging your indebtedness. If quoting other people's actual words, use quotation marks.

The remainder of this section is really intended for more advanced students, e.g. those taking Diplomas, Open University courses or other degrees, where many sources have to be quoted and references documented in a systematic way. If you are not working on such courses you might like to 'skim' this section and refer to it later as the need arises. If you do this, continue working on this Unit with the section on **Abbreviations** on page 57.

One easy and generally accepted way of documenting your references is to include the full reference to your source(s) at the end of

(V) Some essays include clear and specific advice on layout —eg. they ask you to tackle 'the question' in certain sections (eg I survey of the evidence II the problem defined III the experiment. etc. You should, of course, follow any such instructions religiously.

4. (ii) Handwriting

If you write your essays by hand & your writing is hard to read then try the following (taken from Maddox, How To Study, Pan)

   a. Give a specimen of your handwriting to a couple of friends. Ask them to underline any letters, or combinations of letters, which they found difficult to read.

   b. Get your friend to tell you what it is about those underlined sections that cause difficulty —

   eg. words crowded; words joined; loops from one line get tangled up with those of lines above or below.

   c. Analyse your problems in the light of a & b. & take especial care from then on!

your essay in a Bibliography. My Bibliography for this course, for example, would include the following:

Freeman, R. (1972) *How to Study Effectively* – a two month course, National Extension College, Cambridge.
Maddox, H. (1963) *How to Study*, Pan Books, London (Chapter 10 on 'Writing English').

Such references should be listed in alphabetical order, and should contain the author's name, date of publication, the title, and the publisher with place of publication. You might also add a note as to which *parts* of a book you've used (as I do above with Maddox). Then within your text itself you simply put the author and date. Here is an example, from an Open University essay on **Reading**:

Book Selection
Field (1968) and Jones and Buttrey (op. cit.) point out how important it is to observe the developmental stages of selecting books for children. These considerations are also touched on in Gilliland (1970). Disturbingness is another important criterion (1973b Davies).

4.8
(a) What does 'op. cit.' mean?
(b) Why do you suppose there is a 'b' after 1973, for Davies?
(c) What could be said to be missing from the above references?

The above references will be too detailed for many essays, and the convention of recording sources varies slightly from subject to subject, and journal to journal. For more extensive help, see *Theses and Project Work* by C. J. Parsons (Allen and Unwin, 1973) or *How to Write a Research Paper* by R. Berry (Pergamon Press, 1966).

Footnotes: These should be kept to a minimum. You need not record authors in your footnotes, since if you adopt the system recommended above, their names will be gathered together in your Bibliography.

Recording Source References: Give book and line; or act, scene and line; or chapter and page (naming edition used). Here are some examples:

Pope, A. *Epistle to Lord Burlington* l.211.
Shakespeare, W. *Hamlet* V. (i), l.24.
Matthew 6,4*
Jane Austen, *Pride and Prejudice*, chap. 11, p. 201 (Penguin edition).

(Notice that we print the titles of the books in italics to distinguish them. You should use underlining in written work for the same reason.)

* This means Chapter 6, Verse 4.

Normally it's enough to put *'Pride and Prejudice* (p. 201)' after your quotation, as it's obvious from the references listed at the end of your work which book and edition you're referring to. Remember that the aim of naming your sources is to allow your teacher to refer to the appropriate page or passage *himself* if he wishes.

None of the above is intended to be dogmatic: work out a system which makes sense, and suits you and your teacher. Such recording of sources takes time, and is a chore, but it really is an *essential part* of the process and becomes increasingly important as your courses grow more specialized. Best to get into the habit early, rather than find you have to start from scratch at a later date.

Abbreviations

Here are a few which can be useful (not an exhaustive list). You will come across some more in question 5 of the Revision Exercises at the end of this Unit.

b. = born
c. = about (circa) e.g. c. 1900
c. / ch. / chap. = chapter
c.f. / cp. = compare
d. = died
e.g. = for example
ed. = editor
et al. = and others
f. (plural ff.) = and the following – e.g. pp. 100ff means page 100 and pages that follow.
fig. = figure
ibid. = in the same place (i.e. the quotation comes from the place last given as a reference)

N.B. Abbreviations used in your essays should be those generally used. It is not, for example, suitable to use 'etc.' in essays. It's awkward and your teacher can never be sure what the other points are that your etc.' covers!

Remember Unit 1: the essay has to use generally accepted *conventions* in order to communicate with its distant audience. In your notes, on the other hand, you can use any abbreviations, as long as *you* can understand them.

6 A Note on the Requirements of Analytical Writing

In this unit we have dealt with style and detailed matters such as how to start your essay, how to punctuate, and how to spell. But we mustn't lose sight of a wider aspect of style: analytical essays need to be organised according to certain generally accepted criteria. Amongst these are the following:

1. You are expected to provide argument, not just opinion. For example, in the essays on education and capital punishment that you are about to write up, it will not be enough just to give your opinion, as you might in a letter to a friend, or when talking in a pub. You need to *argue* your point, justify it, explain how you arrived at it, provide evidence for it (if possible). *The view itself is of less importance than the way you justify it*. This point is reinforced by some advice given to students of social science: '. . . there is . . . no one "correct" answer . . . but a range of perfectly well-based and acceptable arguments founded on evidence and reasoning.'
2. You try to provide specific examples, illustrations, and references to support your case. You always give any *sources* for your ideas, and you record them in the way described earlier, on p. 25.
3. You remain *relevant* to the question, including only relevant material and indicating clearly *how* it is relevant.
4. You state the *implications* of your points, or of your examples, where this is needed.

7 Assignment D

Read *all* through this section before you start on any part of it.

1. In Assignment B, question 3, you chose an essay topic and collected material for answering it. For Assignment C, question 2 you organised this into a plan. Now turn this plan into an essay of 500–1000 words. Make sure that you remember the advice given in Unit 4 about communicating your ideas clearly on paper. You should try to write a rough draft first.

2. By the end of your work on Assignment C, question 3, you should have made a plan for the essay on capital punishment. Write this plan up as an essay of up to 1000 words. Again, you might well find that a preliminary draft is a good idea.

3. For Assignment F you will be writing an essay on a topic of your own choice. This could be an essay from another subject you are studying. Otherwise choose your own topic. It can be either 'creative' or 'analytical'.

Try, if you can, to make a draft copy first. Before writing up your final copy, ask yourself the following questions (and ask them about each essay you complete from now on!).

Have I:

● Answered the particular question set?

● Broken the question down into separate smaller questions and found answers to them?

● Covered the main aspects?

● Remained relevant throughout?

● Kept to any word limit stated?

● Considered who the reader is and what are his interests and knowledge?

● Made the reader's task as easy as possible?

● Kept to a logical arrangement in the presentation of my ideas?

● Moved smoothly from one point to the next, one section to the next, from paragraph to paragraph, from sentence to sentence?

● Provided enough examples and illustrations of my points?

● Acknowledged my sources and documented them clearly? What kinds of source have I used, primary or secondary? Could I have found better sources?

● Read it aloud to sort out any muddled sentences, mis-spellings, or bad grammar?

● Presented a convincing case which I could justify in a discussion?

8 Revision Exercises

1. 'Writing an essay is a bit like working through a programme on an automatic washing machine'
    (a) because both are purely mechanical processes.
    (b) because the mind has to go through certain processes in a fixed sequence.
Which is more accurate, (a) or (b)?

2. What's wrong with this piece of writing?

This book leads us to imagine a world without machines – or at least – a country and we are left to ask ourselves which one is the best – or is neither better than the other.

3. Which of the following is the odd one out?
Paragraphing is important because:
    (a) It helps the clarity of the argument.
    (b) It shows good planning.
    (c) We talk in paragraphs.

4. Which of these two approaches to the teaching of written expression best represents the view of the author of this course?
   (a) You teach the student 'grammar' and then let him express himself through writing.
   (b) You help the student to think his ideas out clearly first so that he can write lucidly.

5. Give the meaning of each of the following abbreviations:
   (a) no.
   (b) n.
   (c) MS. (plural MSS.)
   (d) m.
   (e) l. (plural ll.)
   (f) i.e.

Answers to Revision Exercises

1. (b) is more accurate than (a).
Essay writing certainly isn't 'purely mechanical' and – for most people– certain stages or problems do seem to occur. You might add: (c) Essays, like washing machines, sometimes go wrong!
2. Loose, careless expression. He can write, but hasn't taken enough time phrasing his points. He expects the teacher to do it for him. Could you rephrase it so that it makes better sense?
3. (c) We don't talk in paragraphs, which are one of the 'artificial' features of writing. Look back to the discussion in Unit 1 which emphasised how important it is to make our writing *explicit* and *logical*.
4. (b) This is *still* a controversial matter. Quite a few teachers would have reservations about my point of view!
5. (a) no. = number
   (b) n. = note
   (c) MS./MSS. = manuscript(s)
   (d) m. = married
   (e) l. (plural ll.) = line (lines)
   (f) i.e. = that is.

Finally, have another look at question 4(b): are you finding for yourself that approach (b) *is* the better one? Has this Unit helped you to feel more confident over matters of written expression? If not, try one of the books suggested in the Bibliography, and talk to your teacher about anything which still worries you.

UNIT 5

Putting it All Together: Writing a Complete Essay

1. Things to look for
2. Assignment E
   the first stage: choice of question
   the second stage: collecting material
   the third stage: making an outline plan
   the fourth stage: writing up
3. Revision exercise
4. Appendix 2: *Spelling: Poor* by Asher Cashdan
5. Appendix 3: Checklist: the main things you need to remember when writing essays

1 Things to Look For

You have now been taken through the various stages. The aim of this Unit is to put them all together in one exercise. In this Unit you will find:

● Assignment E.

● A checklist, to remind you of the points made in earlier Units, and to act as a jog to your memory. (This is shown as Appendix 3, page 73).

2 Assignment E

The essays which you will be required to write for this exercise are of the 'analytical' type. Unfortunately, there is not time to include a creative essay here, but you will have a chance to write a creative essay in Unit 6.

You are being asked to write two essays and you should be able to do the work in about 6 hours. You might need a bit longer, especially if you put in the 'extra optional loop' (i.e. additional sources of information). In an exam, or other situation which makes you concentrate or puts high expectations on your performance, you would be able to do this type of exercise much more quickly.

As Appendix 2 to this Unit you will find an article on spelling reprinted from the magazine *Where*. You will use the material in this article as the basis for both your essays. To make the task manageable, this is the only source which I am giving you: if you wish to make your job longer, more difficult, and also closer to normal essay writing, you can find other sources. This is the 'extra optional loop' which I mentioned above. (To use your local library for this would be valuable experience in source-hunting.)

Go through each of the following stages. (You might need to refresh your memory of the appropriate Units, and also to refer to the check-list at Appendix II.) Before working through the stages, read through the whole of the rest of this Unit so you can see what is involved. Then return to this point to start the work for your Assignment.

The First Stage: Choice of Questions

Choose *two* of the following topics on which to write an essay of not more than 1000 words each. (*Very Important Note: the material will need to be shaped differently to suit the different questions.*)

(a) You are a parent whose 8-year-old child has been defined as 'a poor speller'. Select and discuss the advice given in the article which might help you to take some action.

(b) Discuss the various ways in which teachers approach the teaching of spelling, and evaluate them.

(c) Is poor spelling a 'specific disability'? What might its relationship be to other learning difficulties?

(d) You are preparing a talk for adults who find spelling difficult. Write out your talk, using this article as a basis.

(e) You may make up any question of your own. It should be in some way to do with spelling, and it should use at least some of the material in the article. It should also be a different question from (a), (b), (c), and (d).

You are being given a choice of questions. Choose wisely! – to make the most of your own interests and abilities. This whole first stage – points (a)–(e) above – is the CHOOSING STAGE.

The Second Stage: Collecting Material

Make notes of your work as you do each of the following things. Make them clear enough for your teacher to read.

(a) Analyse your chosen questions carefully. What do they want? What style is appropriate in each case? Underline key words.

(b) Jot down any knowledge/views on each topic you have chosen – i.e. *before* reading the article.

(c) Write down questions to which you will hope to find answers in the passage, or from your own experience. (You might want to amend, add to, or delete these questions in the course of your reading.)

(d) Read the article, and jot down notes that will help you to answer the essay questions you have chosen.

(As an optional extra you could use any other sources of information – books, papers, articles, points from discussion – you may have collected.)

This whole second stage – points (a)–(d) above – is the COLLECTING STAGE. Don't forget the advice you were given earlier on ways of making and storing notes.

The Third Stage: Making an Outline Plan

The previous stage will have left you with material which now needs to be organised into two essay plans. Now make these outline plans. This is the PLANNING STAGE.

The Fourth Stage: Writing Up

Write up the essays, which should each be no more than 1000 words at the very most. This is the WRITING-UP STAGE.

Show your work on stages 1–4 to your teacher. Your *choice* of topics, your *notes*, *outline plan*, and *final version* of the essays form Assignment E.

When you receive your essays back, try to learn from them: follow up any points made by your teacher. Discuss the points with him if necessary. Look things up, extend or expand your ideas as an extra sheet of notes (THE FOLLOWING-UP stage).

Specimen Essays

Here are two essays, by two different students, on two of the topics. Note how the material has been differently shaped to suit the different requirements of each question.

You are Preparing a Talk for Adults Who Find Spelling Difficult. Write Out Your Talk, Using this Article as a Basis

Ladies and gentlemen,

I wonder how many of us put this 'their was' instead of 'there was' when we write a hurried note, or possibly get in a muddle with 'past' and 'passed', 'where' and 'were', 'to' 'too', or 'two'. Unless we are a genius, most of us, at some time, use the wrong spelling in the wrong context.

However, using the wrong word in the wrong context isn't the only reason why we are labelled 'poor spellers'. Do we always hear a word correctly, or do we miss the first spoken letter of a word? Does our brain have difficulty to sort out and organise the signals it receives? My youngest daughter always appeared to miss out the consonants before a vowel. She would call her sister 'eny' instead of 'Wendy'. After considerable hearing tests, which all proved that her hearing was perfect, it was decided that her brain was having difficulty in sorting out the signals it received.

Hearing and speaking the words correctly help towards correct spellings. Obviously, there are the odd words which present difficulties, and one word that readily comes to mind as Wendy has it on her spelling list this week is 'archaeology'. Most words can readily be broken down into smaller words. 'Newspaper' can be broken into two words 'news and paper'; 'whomsoever' can be broken into 'whom so ever'; and 'satisfactory' can be broken into 'sat is fact ory'. We can learn to spell by learning the phonetic sounds of letters of the alphabet. For example, let us take the word 'authoritative'. We break the word up like this 'au th or it a tive'. We recognise letter combinations, and coupled with phonetic sounds, we can learn to spell.

There are basic prefixes and suffixes which we deliberately learn. Can you perhaps tell me some that readily come to mind? Yes, there are '-tion'; 'ing'; 'ent'; 'ph'; 'th'; and 'un' are but a few. Our memory retains combinations of letters. This form of teaching is called structural teaching, and is very popular in junior schools today.

Another method of teaching spelling is the 'Fernald' technique. The word is written out on a piece of paper in large cursive script like this:

You can then trace the shape of the word with a pencil or finger and keep repeating it until it is thoroughly learnt. This method introduces an extra sense, that of movement, which supports auditory and visual skills. Poor listeners and visualisers often make amazing progress learning this technique. The disadvantage with this method is that you cannot generalize the method to all words; only particular words which are being learnt.

Reading obviously helps with spelling. Don't read the sexy magazines or comic strips, then give up. Read newspapers; not only the gossip columns, but the political news and what is happening world-wide. Choose a good newspaper if possible, such as *The Times* or *The Guardian*, and study their use of words.

In summing up this talk I want to stress one thing; believe in yourself. Believe that you can spell. Once you believe in yourself, anything is possible; and that includes spelling. If you find that you cannot hear a word properly, ask your GP to refer you to the local hospital for hearing tests. Start to approach spelling by choosing goals that are within your grasp. When you have achieved what you set out to learn, you will be so pleased that you will set your sights higher. Why don't a group of you organise a sponsored 'Spell-in'? Perhaps the proceeds could be donated to a local charity? I hope this talk has given you some encouragement to try and improve your spelling.

Discuss the Various Ways in which Teachers Approach the Teaching of Spelling and Evaluate Them

There appears to have been more controversy over the teaching of spelling than over any other subject. On the one hand, devotees of each particular system claim that theirs is the only possible way to achieve results, and on the other, critics argue that standards have fallen abysmally. There have been many would-be reformers, notable among them being George Bernard Shaw, who left a large amount of money towards spelling reform, and who was scathing in his condemnation of the alphabet. In 1837 Isaac Pitman designed the Initial Teaching Alphabet; this was revised in recent years by his grandson, Sir James Pitman, and has been used in some schools since 1961. The two other most widely taught systems are the 'look-and-say' method and the alphabet and phonetics approach.

The i.t.a. is a forty-four character alphabet which attaches one sound only to each written symbol, and Pitman's hypothesis was that once the child was able to read by the i.t.a. he would have no difficulty in transferring his skill to traditional orthography. To this end, the i.t.a. letters, especially their upper halves, were kept as similar as possible to t.o., for research has shown that it is chiefly by the upper halves of letters that we recognize them. Keith Gardner in *Towards Literacy* points out an obvious pitfall of the system when he states that it is extremely difficult to justify writing in i.t.a. 'Here one form of spelling is learnt, consolidated by practice and hammered home by repetition; all to be discarded at a later date. There are obvious dangers here if teachers consider that the attainment of accurate spelling is part of early education. It is indisputable that early habits are difficult to eradicate.' Another critic points out that the system was adopted because it was thought it would make it easier for the child to learn by removing the complexities from what he learns, instead of concentrating on making it as easy as possible for him to master those complexities. The child might have little difficulty in reading the new language but he then had to begin trying to visualize the new spelling, with all its oddities. He would find this doubly difficult, because the i.t.a. has probably encouraged him to spell words from their sounds, rather than from the way they look, and because he has not been able to store up mental images of irregular words, or of most words as they are normally spelled.

The phonetics method uses the sound of the letters of the alphabet, i.e. A, Buh, Kuh, Duh, and so on, as opposed to their names, i.e. Ay, Bee, See, Dee, and so on. Great confusion can be caused in a child's mind if he is first taught the names, for when he tries to use phonetics in his reading he is constantly confused between the *names* of the letters and their *sounds*. A fairly large number of words can be worked out by the child if he has grasped the sounds of the letters. Once this individual letter stage is passed then the child goes on to learn the sounds of the various vowel combinations.

However, even with a knowledge of phonetics, there are some words that cannot be worked out, e.g. here, why, our, your, there. The 'look-and-say' method is useful here and quite often these two systems are taught side by side. Here the child sees the same word over and over again and by so doing it is hoped that he will continue to recognize it wherever it is met in subsequent reading. In other words, the shape of the word, the way it looks, receives more emphasis than the corresponding sound. Most reading experts take the view that to rely on phonics alone or on 'look-and-say' alone produces under-achievement in the pupil.

Felicity Hughes taught her two and three year old daughters to read by the Glenn Doman method, which uses the 'whole-word' approach, coupled with phonics, and she asserts that children taught by her method will have little difficulty with spelling. She states: 'The child who spells well is not the child who has learned a great many rules about spelling, but the child who reads a lot. Almost without thinking about it he visualizes the words he needs, and when he has written them, he can tell whether or not they look right. So we can assume that the way a child sees words as he reads plays quite a large part in the way he spells them.'

Adams and Pearce, in their book *The English Teacher*, also advocate extensive reading, coupled with word-gaming, and 'hooking-up' written language to speech. They conclude that 'a policy of saturating children in written-text-brought-to-sound and spoken-language-brought-to-page will be far more productive than reliance on rules or rote-learnings of spellings'. However, they agree that there is a place for rote learning in dealing with children's mistakes which are of three distinct kinds: new words not yet mastered; habitual errors (which could be caused by the 'look-and-say' method and need spelling tests and rote learning to correct); and carelessness or haste. Old-fashioned spelling tests can be used inventively, for example, by asking pupils to use a collection of mis-spelled words in any order in a story, or by an affixation game where as many suffixes and prefixes are attached as the root word will bear.

Jones and Mulford in *Children Using Language* find it desirable that the learning of spelling should be separated to some extent from composition. They suggest a teacher looks with each child, intensively and systematically for a few minutes twice a week, at words and families of words that the child has had difficulty with; sometimes this will be best done with a pair or group of children. They also suggest that a child learns by rote spellings from a personal spelling book, and then tests himself with the help of a friend, for five minutes each day. They add that there is also a place for occasional word games that have the aim of establishing spelling regularities and irregularities but the important thing is that the procedures adopted should become neither a burden nor a distraction.

The use of dictionaries is advocated by many experts. C. T. Hawker's *Spell It Yourself* is neither a dictionary nor a conventional spelling book but lists 8000 root words, past and present participles and derivatives, but no definitions. He argues that in written compositions children use words whose meanings they understand: they do not often need definitions of the words they cannot spell. Children's ability to read and recognize words is much greater than their ability to spell them. In general, he says, children learn best by finding out for themselves and this leads to correct spelling and increased written vocabulary.

From the foregoing, it would appear that although i.t.a. could be useful in teaching very backward children, it could cause confusion, and that a combination of 'look-and-say' and phonics is desirable, with a place for some rote learning, reading and the imaginative use of dictionaries and word games. The different approaches should be complementary rather than competitive. Adams and Pearce emphasize that because all subjects of the curriculum are conducted in English they are also in some measure teaching English. They point out the unrealistic expectations of teachers who never correct mis-spellings in pupils' work in their own subjects, but are outspoken in the staffroom about how English teachers are falling down on the job. 'Children who "are not taught to spell nowadays" are being "not taught" by a majority of their teachers'. This would seem to be a justifiable statement, and the whole matter is summed up neatly in their conclusion: 'In the long run, however, children will spell if their teachers make clear that good spelling is one of the things they expect. To expect anything less in a society which attaches weight to spelling, is to deceive them about the real world.'

Bibliography

Wilkinson, Andrew (1971) *The Foundation of Language*. OUP (Chapter IX, Media and Schemes – 1.3 Simplified Spelling).

Gardner, Keith (1970) *Towards Literacy*. Blackwell (Appendix I on i.t.a.).

Hughes, Felicity (1971) *Reading and Writing Before School*. Jonathan Cape (Chapter 8 on Spelling).

Adams, Anthony and Pearce, John (1977) *Every English Teacher*. OUP (Chapter 8 'Points of Debate – A Policy for Spelling', Chapter 9 'Theories and Attitudes – English, Language and the School').

Jones, Anthony and Mulford, Jeremy (1971) *Children Using Language*. OUP (Spelling, etc., pages 153–174).

Hawker, G. T. (1975) *Spell It Yourself*. OUP (Note for Teachers, p. 116).

Appendix 2: 'Spelling: Poor' *by Asher Cashdan*

How do you decide that your child is hopeless at spelling? It may be from the bald entry on his report form. Or perhaps you find him struggling with his thank-you letter to Grannie: 'How *do* you spell "swimming" – one "m" or two?' Surely he ought to know that by his age? Or perhaps you pick up one of his school books and find a vast number of spelling mistakes. The teacher may have corrected them and the whole page is disfigured with crossings out. More often the work is uncorrected and one wonders whether the teacher has even seen all those dreadful mistakes.

Just as with physical ailments at earlier stages, parents want to know whether the mistakes matter or are simply inevitable at this stage, how long a child will take to learn to spell better and what help (if any) they can give themselves. Most important they want to know whether the child is having reading difficulties – which he will not grow out of (or not without special help) – and whether these difficulties are going to interfere with his whole educational future and career prospects. Some of these questions can be answered quite quickly; the rest will need rather more careful examination.

Is help necessary?
The first problem is finding out whether the spelling trouble is transient and trivial or whether it is more serious. This should be discussed with the class teacher or the school head as soon as doubts arise. Parent-teacher relations are not always perfect, but teachers should always be prepared to discuss a child helpfully provided that they are not made to feel that the parent is criticising the teaching, or being over-fussy.

Normal development of spelling
Let's go back to the beginning of the child's school career and see how his reading, writing and spelling develop. Nowadays your children are encouraged to write down their thoughts as soon as they have sufficient interest and motor skill. They write stories, news, invitations, letters and messages well before they are fluent readers.

Naturally they have a constant need to use words which they cannot yet spell or even read. The result is that many infants seem to develop their own personal spelling system – so idiosyncratic and inconsistent that much of what they write cannot be read either by adults or (except from memory) by the child himself.

The old-fashioned teacher might well have discouraged this sort of writing until the child had built up a bigger vocabulary of words he could read and spell, and would have corrected all his mistakes by striking out offending words and having him copy each one out correctly three, five, ten or twenty times.

The modern approach is much more relaxed. The teacher recognises that at the infant stage (and for some time afterwards) it is the content, rather than the form, of what the child has to say that really matters and she is careful not to kill the child's interest and enthusiasm by an undue emphasis on tidiness, handwriting and spelling. As a result the uncorrected book, while it occasionally signals poor organisation and sloppiness on the teacher's part, is more likely to reflect a deliberate and sensible policy.

Some children (of, say, five to seven), are likely then to produce quantities of written work full of uncorrected spelling mistakes. At first sight this might suggest that standards in spelling are lower than formerly, but this is probably not so. What we are seeing is simply a greater output from young children, both in quantity and in diversity of written vocabulary, and hence a large number of spelling mistakes which will disappear as they grow older. But as we shall see, they will not disappear on their own – appropriate teaching will be needed.

Another source of puzzlement to parents is the young child who makes really 'wild' mistakes. If a child wrote 'yot' for 'yacht', this would be wrong but meaningful, but what about the child who writes 'sbxp'? In fact the second child is showing the helplessness when in doubt of those who have been started on reading with look-and-say (or 'sight') methods and who have not been given any 'phonic training'. The child has been taught to concentrate on the whole word, rather than the individual letters that make it up. All the child can do then is try to remember the visual pattern of the word. He has no way of checking his work until he begins to learn about the sound values of individual letters and letter combinations. The child who wrote 'sbxp' was, of course, vaguely remembering the word 'ship' which he had seen under the picture of a yacht. Children who are taught to read purely by sight methods and not given systematic phonic training or spelling instruction are being taught on the assumption that they will pick it up by themselves. This is what Margaret Peters is getting at in the title of her book *Spelling: Caught or Taught?* (Routledge, a good survey with plenty of useful advice). On the basis of her own and other people's researches she comes to the firm conclusion that most children *do not* 'catch' spelling, but have to be taught.

Fortunately very few teachers do use purely sight methods and virtually all schools do make a point of teaching children to spell, though they vary greatly in the amount of time and skill they spend on this aspect of school work. And a few otherwise very good teachers scorn to spend much time on spelling, associating it with old fashioned formal teaching which was concerned with form to the almost total exclusion of content. They may sometimes forget, as Margaret Peters argues forcefully, that the child who has learnt to spell well and without any thought is much freer to write creatively than the one who is always having to stop and worry about whether he has got it right. The latter child may even avoid using the words that he really wants in favour of shorter, simpler words whose spelling he knows he will get right.

Part of the problem is that we have a firm convention in this country that there is only one permissible way of spelling virtually every word in the language. This rule is of relatively recent standing and although useful has perhaps been carried to excess. There is no doubt that without a reasonable standardization of spelling, learning to read and write would become progressively harder and eventually communication would break down. But there is also a certain amount of social snobbery about 'good' spelling so that even mild and innocent variations are heavily stamped on.

Attainment in spelling
The advantage of this rigidity about spelling is that it makes it possible for us to measure children's attainment in spelling in much the same way as we test their reading and mathematical attainments. We can thus assign 'spelling ages' to children. An eight year old might have a spelling age of seven – this would make him one year behind, meaning that his attainment in spelling was similar to that of the average seven year old.

Such a discrepancy would be of little importance. As a rule of thumb we consider that junior school children have to be at least two years behind in spelling before they have anything of a problem. It is important also to note that in comparing children with the average standard of their own or a younger age group, we are tacitly accepting that the average standard is the desirable one. In fact we might consider that standards in general are either very high or very low; in my opinion they are quite high enough. Nevertheless attainment tests in spelling (usually consisting of oral dictation of single words) are useful as a *preliminary* to the use of diagnostic tests for those with special difficulties; especially as under normal circumstances most children retain their relative place on the test over quite long periods.

There is a close but not a complete relationship between the child's attainments in spelling and reading. Obviously a child who can hardly read is not likely to be able to spell well, but the reverse is also true. Some poor spellers read very well, but they are far from common. Where the child is a good reader the spelling difficulty is likely to be minor rather than severe.

How they teach spelling

Just as with reading, so with spelling teachers vary widely in their methods of teaching. Some follow a particular textbook method very closely, others use a mixture of methods, and some do not seem to 'teach' the subject at all. At one extreme are those who set a list of anything up to a dozen words daily for the children to learn and be tested on. At its worst this list consists of a jumble of unrelated words, many of them beyond the child's comprehension, their only unity lying perhaps in the fact that they all begin with 'a' one week, 'b' the next and so on through the alphabet. At its best the list is planned so as to contain words which are meaningful to the child and are grouped in such a way as to teach him structural relationships; for example, town, brown, flower. The child is rarely taught *how* to learn the list and he struggles with it as best he can.

Other methods are more individual and child-centred. The child may make his own dictionary of words he has mis-spelled or he may 'collect' new words, learn them individually and add them to a stock which he keeps in a special box file.

Again the spelling work may be confined to the 'English lesson' or used as a general policy whenever the child is reading or writing or simply hearing new words.

Freak spellers

Highly specific disability in spelling is relatively rare. A child who seems a poor speller may on investigation turn out either to be quite reasonable for his age, or to have other difficulties as well as the spelling one. It may prove that the symptom noticed by the parent is only one of many; it may not even be the most severe of the child's difficulties. In other words, a child who is obviously backward at spelling may turn out to be more in need of help with his reading than simply of extra spelling lessons. Or he may want neither of these but need speech therapy.

Spelling difficulties can be caused by a variety of factors. Some of these are subtle; but it is quite possible to miss obvious sources of trouble by looking immediately for unusual difficulties. Thus a child who has defective sight or hearing may have serious trouble in spelling. It is much easier to read a word or sentence which one has seen only hazily, using contextual and other clues, than it is to write the words down oneself. Furthermore some children have minor visual and auditory defects, which do not handicap them in everyday life and can be missed at routine examinations, but which make it difficult for them to learn to spell. So any child who has serious difficulty in spelling ought to have a thorough medical check-up, paying special attention to vision, hearing and speech. Such a child might turn out to have a high-frequency hearing loss. This could mean that he consistently mishears certain speech sounds (such as a final 's') although his deafness might hardly show in other respects. With a suitable hearing aid he might make considerable progress.

Perceptual problems

Accurate spelling depends on hearing and seeing properly and to some extent on speaking correctly also. But some children who have no difficulties in these respects nevertheless spell words as if they were hearing or seeing them badly. In their case the defect is not in one of the sense organs, but rather in the brain's ability to sort out and organise the signals it receives from the sense organs. Such children have what psychologists call 'perceptual' difficulties. These difficulties may in a few cases be constitutional and due to specific neurological disturbances or immaturity: that is, the brain disturbance affects only those skills needed for spelling. In far more cases, however, the perceptual difficulties may be linked to the child's past history – he may never have learned systematic perceptual habits or he may have learned bad ones.

Sequencing
Some children who have trouble in analyzing words and spelling them correctly are having difficulty with what one might call the 'time-and-motion' side of spelling. Words are not just static symbols; they represent a sequence of sounds moving in a fixed direction across the paper. Some children have particular difficulty in handling this dimension of spelling. They see and hear words accurately, but when they come to write them down, they move from right to left (writing 'saw' for 'was', 'no' for 'on'), or they put the letters down with almost no regard for order at all (as in 'flain' for 'final'). Such children may be particularly helped by a multisensory approach, as we shall soon explain.

The child's image of himself as a speller
As with any other aspects of school work, the child's disabilities may reflect his relationships with other people, the climate in which he has been taught and the habits and attitudes he has acquired. A child may spell badly because he has missed schooling or because spelling has been much stressed by a teacher or parent with whom he got on badly. The more established the bad spelling has become, the harder it is to retrain the child. However it would be a mistake to consider, even with awkward children, that the difficulty is a kind of shamming and that the child has only to 'snap out of it'. Emotional attitudes and intellectual skills are so interwoven that one very rarely finds a case where only one of these is involved.

This is particularly the case with spelling (and indeed with those who consider themselves unable to do arithmetic). What is at stake is the child's image of himself as a speller. Once the child feels that he is poor at spelling, he expects to make mistakes and he despairs of ever getting straight. Once this point has been reached, and it is a very common situation with children and adults who are simply 'weak' spellers, the situation very rarely improves by itself. Progress will only be made when the person can be convinced that he is capable of becoming a competent speller and given systematic help.

Getting help
If the teacher cannot solve the problem by herself the child should be seen by a remedial teacher or an educational psychologist. Both of these are in relatively short supply but almost every local authority employs one or both, and even if they are unable to give a child personal tuition they should at least be able to see him once or twice and advise the teachers and parents. If your authority has no appropriate staff (or, as is more common, is very under-staffed) it should send your child to the nearest child guidance clinic or remedial centre even if it is out of the area – and pressure should be brought to bear on the authority to improve its facilities.

The clinic should be able to arrange any necessary medical examinations through the school health service (or this could be done through your GP). It should carry out at least a preliminary diagnosis, and help get treatment started. If the clinic (or remedial teacher) decides to help your child, you should discuss your part with them – should you practise with the child, how often and in what way? If they suggest that you do nothing, don't worry; they may feel that the child will do better under less pressure. It can be very difficult for parents to teach their own children without resentments growing up (on both sides!) and tensions increasing.

An adult with a problem will not often come to an expert for help unless he is strongly motivated to improve and he is, therefore, likely to be co-operative. With children the reverse is the case. They are usually brought for help by their parents or teachers, and the first task of the remedial specialist is to help the child to see the purpose and need for improvement and to make him realise that he *can* improve. Thus both teacher and parent have to be concerned with reshaping the child's attitudes and motivation, and with giving him the experience of success – the best of all motivators. So she starts right at the beginning at a level where success is certain and builds up slowly from there. Lessons should ideally be short, related to the child's interests, and frequent. An hour's mechanical instruction once a week is of very little help even when carried out by an expert.

Kinaesthetic training

The child who has not learned how to spell must self-consciously establish systematic habits if he is to overcome his difficulties. One method is to use as many sensory channels as possible in learning a new word or a word which has been spelt wrongly. The child should not be shown the wrong spelling; he should concentrate only on the correct one. He looks at the word, sounds it out and follows its shape with finger or pencil. Using this technique, usually called the kinaesthetic or Fernald technique (after Grace Fernald who popularized it), the word is written out on a piece of paper in large cursive script so that the child can follow it with his finger without any breaks. The child can then test himself or be tested by writing out the word and then repeating the word until it is thoroughly learnt. Words should not normally be spelt aloud (letter by letter) by either pupil or teacher as this process is of little help and distracts attention from the actual sound of the word.

The strength of this method is that it introduces the extra sense, that of movement, to support the child's auditory and visual skills. Children who are poor listeners and visualisers often make amazing progress with this method. It also has the advantage of using words which the child selects himself as ones he wishes to write. The disadvantage is that it only helps with the particular words being learnt and provides the child with little basis for making generalizations to other words.

Structural teaching

So many children need instead (or as well) some systematic structural teaching – deliberate learning of common endings such as -tion, -ough, and so on, the learning of common prefixes and suffixes, practice with word families, with breaking words into syllables, breaking words down completely and building them up again. Sometimes they need help in building up their visual memory span, that is the number of letters and letter combinations that they can take in and retain at one time; a task in which flash cards can often be of great help. Above all the child needs to be taught learning techniques as well as how to test himself. A good technique often is to look at the word, cover it, write the whole word, look again, cover it again, write the word, and so on. Structurally classified lists of words are of obvious help here, and through them the child can be taught the sequential probabilities of English words (less technically, the common English letter patterns and sequences).

The remedial plan
In a particular case, a close analysis of the child's characteristic mistakes, coupled with a little experimentation with him, will tell the remedial expert which aspects of perception and execution the child is weakest at and enable her to devise a combination of the above teaching methods for use with the child, based on his particular difficulties and his preferred modes of learning.

But here we are talking of the child with special difficulties. As we have already suggested, most cases of spelling difficulty need never arise. If the child's and the teacher's attitudes are healthy and spelling is taught systematically but neither too soon nor too formally, then only a small number of cases will require such specialist attention. As with many other educational problems, larger issues come into the picture. These include adequate contact between parents and teachers, the ratio of teachers to pupils, the quality of teacher-training and so on.

The Sponsored Spell
Why not take up this novel idea for encouraging reluctant spellers and help a really worthwhile cause at the same time? Draw up a list of 50 words from which your children and their friends can choose 25 to be tested on on an arranged day. The 'volunteer spellers' can then get as many people as possible to sponsor them with a certain amount of money for each word they spell correctly in the test. Shirley Augustus at the Invalid Children's Aid Association, which is raising money in this way, says it can be organised at any time and by anyone.

Reprinted from WHERE, the education magazine for parents, published by the Advisory Centre for Education.

Appendix 3: Checklist: The Main Things You Need to Remember When Writing Essays

1. Approaching the Essay
(These points are discussed in Units 1 and 2)

● Knowledge of your own strengths and weaknesses.

● Knowledge of your course generally and the demands it makes.

● Awareness of what's involved in *written* communication.

- Preparedness to take time *thinking*.

- A positive approach: you expect to enjoy the process, and to do it well. You don't view writing an essay as a mystery or as a chore.

2. Examining the Question
(These points are discussed in Unit 2)

- Awareness of the kind of essay set (analytical or creative).

- Knowledge of what makes a 'good' essay within each type.

- Ability to recognise key words and to understand exactly what these demand of you.

- Ability to work out what is relevant and what is not.

3. Collecting or Generating Material
(These points are discussed in Unit 2)

- Ability to collect material that is *relevant*.

- Ability to collect in a systematic way (e.g. by formulating questions *before* you start to read).

- Keeping records of sources you use.

- Using a *variety* of sources.

- Taking notes effectively.

- *Thinking* all the time.

4. Planning the Essay Outline
(These points are discussed in Unit 3)

- Realizing why it is important to plan.

- Awareness of possible ways of planning.

- Ability to select main points (not too many) and to allow enough space to develop and illustrate them.

- Preparedness to *discard* material if necessary.

- Realizing possible pitfalls in writing introductions and conclusions.

5. Writing up the Essay
(These points are discussed in Unit 4)

Have I:

- Answered the particular question set?

- Broken the question down into separate smaller questions and found answers to them?

- Covered the main aspects?

- Remained relevant throughout?

- Kept to any word limit stated?

- Considered who the reader is and what are his interests and knowledge?

- Made the reader's task as easy as possible?

- Kept to a logical arrangement in the presentation of my ideas?

- Moved smoothly from one point to the next, one section to the next, from paragraph to paragraph, from sentence to sentence?

- Provided enough examples and illustration of my points?

- Acknowledged my sources and documented them clearly? What kinds of source have I used, primary or secondary? Could I have found better sources?

- Read it aloud, to sort out any muddled sentences, mis-spellings or bad grammar?

- Presented a convincing case which I could justify in a discussion?

6. Learning from the Essay
(These points are discussed in Unit 6)

Ability to learn from your teacher's comments, e.g.:

- Comments which acknowledge your point of view or stage of development.

- Comments suggesting new ideas, fresh examples, different opinions.

- Simple corrections of facts, or mistakes.

- Comments aimed at helping you to make your written expression clearer.

- Comments guiding you to the proper use of evidence.

- Comments which evaluate your essay as a whole, which will probably involve the giving and justifying of a grade or mark.

- Comments on *detailed* aspects of your structure.

- Comments looking back at work you've done earlier, or at difficulties you might encounter in work to come.

UNIT 6

Learning From Essays

1. Things to look for
2. Another look at the word 'essay'
3. Student learning: a case study
4. Some final comments on this case study
5. Assignment F
6. Postscript: essays and examinations

1 Things to Look For

After working through this Unit and carrying out the related activities, you should be able to:

● Think of the essay in all its stages as a means to further your own learning.

● Work out ways in which you yourself can build up a dialogue with *your* teacher.

2 Another Look at the Word 'Essay'

You know by now what an 'essay' is and you have been writing some. But the word 'essay' has another shade of meaning and this is relevant for us now.

Here are some definitions of 'an essay' (i.e. the noun) and 'to essay' (i.e. the verb) taken from the *Oxford English Dictionary*. Read them through and then think about what they seem to have in common.

Noun: the action or process of trying or testing
an attempt or endeavour
a first attempt in learning or practice
a tentative effort

Verb: to put to the test
to attempt anything difficult
to set oneself to do something

It boils down to 'try' doesn't it? An essay is a *try* at something *difficult*. We as students are, by definition, *trying to learn* something; to do something at present beyond us. We are putting ourselves to the test, and the 'essays' are invaluable as evidence of how well we are doing in this subject; i.e. they are for *our own* guidance. Properly seen, the assessment is an indication to us of our progress; it has a positive function. Remember above all, we are competing only against ourselves.

In any course you study you should make sure that:

● You understand what you are aiming at, what is expected of you, what skills you are trying to learn, and what knowledge you are expected to master.

● You understand from each assignment how far you are progressing and what you should concentrate on next.

● You are acquiring the ability to be self-critical in a constructive way.

We do these things quite naturally in many daily activities, e.g. in putting up a shelf, playing a game of football, or planning a journey. In these, we know what we are aiming at and the standards we are working towards; all we need to do is to apply this approach to our studies. It all comes down to a question of our *attitudes*. As we prepare the material for our essays, we are being forced to organise our thoughts clearly and communicate them to a distant reader. We might think we grasp a subject, but doing an essay will help us make sure since it tests a very wide range of skills and understanding – e.g. the exact formulation of difficult concepts, and the ability to convey a complex logical argument.

3 Student Learning: A Case Study

Most students can *talk* to their teachers, so they have the chance to discuss their essays together with an expert. This isn't always possible, though, so teachers have to write comments on the essays their students hand in. It's very important to learn from these comments.

In this case study I would like you to follow an actual example of a student in the Open University 'learning by correspondence'. Because the student will not see his teacher, he must learn all he can from the comments written on his work. The essay is taken from a third level literature course (A302), but you can see the general processes of teaching and learning at work even though you may have no knowledge of the book under discussion. (It is, in fact, *Heart of Darkness* by Joseph Conrad.)

> **6.1**
> Study the question which is set out below and identify the 'key words'.

Imagine that the year is 1902. You have always been a great reader of novels – Austen, Dickens, George Eliot, the Brontës – though you have had some difficulties with more 'modern' authors. Now one of your grown-up children insists that you should try a work by an author previously unknown to you: *Heart of Darkness*. Write a part of a letter describing your response to it. (In approximately 1500 words.)

When you have read the **Discussion** of the above question, read the essay below, submitted by a student. Try to read this as quickly as you can, noticing the *approach* the student adopts to the question rather than the details of the subject matter.

Make a note of the places where the student is identifying the 'key words' which you indicated in question 2.

My dearest Daughter,
I did appreciate your kind thought in sending me a copy of 'The Heart of Darkness' by Joseph Conrad. As you so often say there is such pleasure in reading and I am delighted that the encouragement I gave you all those years ago has been of benefit. My gratitude is tempered by my disappointment at not enjoying it as much as I had hoped.
I suppose my difficulties began because I was not fully prepared to accept the way the story was told. I have reservations about the style of narration and about the way the narration is 'placed' in another setting. I accept Marlow as the narrator, but I am puzzled as to why Conrad thought it necessary to have another narrator introduce Marlow, and I am certainly unsure of the relationship between the author, the first narrator and Marlow. Since I know little of the first narrator I have no yardstick to judge his comments on Marlow, which should be significant – or should they? After all, it is he who queries whether the meanings of a sailor's story should be internal or external and this does affect my acceptance of Marlow's story. My view of Marlow could be drawn entirely from what he says, thinks and does, (or more accurately, what he says he said, says he thought and says he did!) but I have a constant nagging doubt engendered by the first narrator and by some of the links, e.g. 'Try to be civil, Marlow' (p. 57) that there is more to him that I need to know. Perhaps it is only through a lifetime's familiarity with their work but I believe I can relate and identify Austen, Eliot and Dickens through their control of the narration (though I would be the first to admit that Emily Brontë is very complex in this respect) whereas modern writers seem to confuse the issue. How much about Henry James does Maisie know or reveal? Is it Jude or Hardy that is really 'obscure'? More particularly who is Conrad? Can he achieve distance and perspective by viewing himself as Marlow through the other narrator? Or is it that Conrad as the first narrator is seeing himself in the character of Marlow as he has become through the power of experience, rather than as he was?
This confusion is made worse for me because of the placing of the narrators in the setting on the Thames. I can appreciate that the juxtaposition of its calm and order against the chaos of the Congo does have a dramatic effect but the puzzling anonymity of the five people on the 'Nellie' is in such direct contrast to the details about those on the Congo that unity seems to be lost. In addition there seems a definite (but deliberate) stylistic difference between

the attractive past of the Thames – 'ships whose names are like jewels flashing in the night of time' – and the awful present of the Congo, which is, for me, too emphatic to convince.

Although there is a sequence of actions and events which can be called the story it appears that what I am being asked to do as reader is not just accompany Marlow in his search for Kurtz, but rather share with Marlow his discovery of himself. In these modern novels there seems to be a need for something far beyond mere reading which I suppose one could call a depth of perception and this demands a great deal from the reader. I am fully aware that Conrad is consciously and deliberately choosing his words to 'lead me' in a similar way to the authorial comments of earlier novels. The limited length of the book means that, although there are fewer words, more references and meanings are compressed into them, and I am not really sure that I understand all the links and connected ideas. Since I believe that the novel should be capable of standing on its own, I expect the novelist to supply me with all the 'keys' I require.

I think Conrad is seeking to expand horizons not merely in a technical sense but also by examining central themes and placing emphasis on unusual settings. The book does examine the theme of Imperialism (Colonialism!) and suggests that in the clash between Western civilisation and that of Africa there is much that is dubious about the practical realities, irrespective of whatever principles are being extolled. I will admit that most of the earlier novels I admire examine only parts of the society rather than discuss central issues. Perhaps Conrad wishes to make an objective comment on these issues and thus tries to preserve his separateness from Marlow. But the latter is affected – almost overwhelmed – by his experiences and I assume we should be involved too. By his concentration on the limited number of characters Conrad does make it possible for the reader to see the central and broader themes, but it is in the balancing of reality (as identified by Marlow) and the symbolic (as created by Conrad) that I find the greatest difficulty.

Of course symbolism plays an important part in earlier novels but here Conrad by continuous emphasis on, for example, the concept of darkness and evil, may make the reader forget the real darkness and evil that exist. The problem with symbolism is that it may be misunderstood (or not understood at all) and this inevitably means that there are loose ends which I expect the author to tie together. To give one fundamental example: darkness/blackness is found throughout the book. In London (p. 6), by 'those who tackle a darkness' (p. 9), the quarrel over two black hens (p. 12), the black wool for knitting (pp. 15 and 16), 'the jungle so dark as to be almost black' (p. 20), white men with black moustaches (p. 33), and of course many, many others concluding with 'the black bank of clouds' and the 'heart of immense blackness' (p. 132). But what is this darkness/blackness? It is not just evil, or the Congo, or Black Africa, or Negroes, or Colonialism, or mystery, or death. It is partly all of these but as I try to perceive it, it seems also to be the areas of the mind that I as reader cannot understand because neither Conrad, nor Marlow, (nor Kurtz) understand them either. One thing that does seem to me to be crucial is the title and concept of the 'Heart of Darkness'. Since the 'heart' and 'life' are in many ways synonymous, is Conrad implying that if we understand the very spring from which the darkness flows we could understand everything?

I am puzzled – perhaps unsatisfied is a better phrase – by certain other features of the novel. There is a vagueness which seems to have no purpose except perhaps to create vagueness. Thus the crew of the 'Nellie' are identified by the titles of what they do (except Marlow) rather than by naming them. Similarly 'the Intended' is not identified further though I agree that this ambivalence reminds us of the idealized and idolized concept of Kurtz that she has created in memory of him. There is confusion also in the way we approach Marlow's story, brought about by the comments of the first narrator and phrases such as 'we were fated to hear about one of Marlow's inconclusive experiences' which implies he has told other tales. Is this one out of the ordinary? Marlow himself becomes confused (p. 31) and one must ask if this happens elsewhere.

My final impressions must depend on how I see the death of Kurtz. Marlow believes that Kurtz broke through the heart of darkness during that 'supreme moment of complete knowledge', but he is already ill himself and his comments on life (are they what he thought or what he is thinking?) are inconclusive. But clearly Marlow (and Conrad) are obsessed by Fate or Destiny – call it what you like – but it is clearly dark to them also. Thus Conrad (with his love of adjectival qualification) reflects through Marlow on life as that 'mysterious arrangement of merciless logic for a futile purpose'. Marlow believes that Kurtz's 'the horror, the horror' is a moral victory, presumably because he has accepted the truth of what he has seen and done. Kurtz is remarkable to Marlow because 'he had something to say and said it' and Marlow shows himself to be truly ordinary when he lies to the Intended for Marlow does *not* say it. Perhaps the whole conclusion is deeply ironic for surely 'His end was in every way worthy of his life' cannot be interpreted in any other way. Is the reflection of irony present in the listeners on the 'Nellie' who are either overwhelmed or disinterested? Is the final paragraph the ultimate irony in that wherever the 'Nellie' goes, life will lead to the heart of darkness? As you can see your Conrad raises the questions but I cannot find the answers.

Perhaps when I said at the beginning of this letter that I did not 'enjoy' the novel I may have misjudged my approach. Perhaps enjoyment is only a part of the process and perhaps I did not give enough of myself. I did appreciate the conscious effort and the technical skill of the writing and I do believe the effort to extend the horizons of the novel is to be welcomed. But the difficulties outweighed the assets.

Thank you again for sending the novel. Perhaps it is wrong for me to judge Conrad on the basis of this novel alone but you did ask for my opinion and as you know I am always pleased to give that.

Your loving father

The essay itself is an 'imagined letter' communicating 'a response' – and you will have found many of the key words directly quoted e.g. 'difficulties', 'great reader of novels', 'modern writers'.

6.2

Try to *evaluate* the essay in terms of essay writing – rather than in terms of its subject matter. Ask yourself the questions posed in the Checklist at the end of Unit 5, i.e. Has he . . . ? *Don't spend too long on this.* Then look carefully at the annotated essay and **Discussion.**

Now read the tutor's completed Grading Comment Form (which accompanied the essay):

I think you deserve an 'A' here. I like the creative choice of situation and tone (father to daughter). This gives you suitable scope for an analysis of the tale in very much the way the questions demands. You don't waste time, either, on inessentials; but you go straight to important questions, both about Conrad and the modern novel. Once or twice your points could have been more clearly expressed or more fully elaborated but, on the other hand, they are difficult points to get clearly and fully articulated in a short essay of this kind.

6.3

In this comment, does the tutor: (a) Say why he thinks this is good? (b) Indicate possible weaknesses? Quote any relevant part of his comment in your answer.

6.4

From the tutor's comments *on the essay itself* (page 98) pick out: (a) Three examples of praise by the tutor confirming points the student has made. (b) Two examples of the tutor suggesting extensions to the points the student has made. (c) Two examples of the tutor faulting style or organisation.

However the learning process did not stop with the completion of the essay. In a letter to the tutor, the student explained how he had come to write the essay, and how demanding it had been:

My main purpose however in writing is to comment on the way I tackled A 302 09. I must hasten to add that this is no apology but an attempt to explain my approach and of course has nothing to do with the marking.

In general I have written essays for assignments which, no matter how objective they seek to be, are almost always personal statements of what the novel means to me. In A 302 09 I chose to do an essay where I was writing for someone else, and many of the statements I have made there, I profoundly disagree with.

I tried to get inside the mind of the father of 1902 and feel what I think he felt. I wrote the essay three times – the first was a very negative father who could not understand and did not wish to! This was *too* negative and so in the modified version the father accepted the novel but could not understand it. In the third and final one I tried to give an idea of the father having difficulties yet showing understanding based on his previous knowledge of novels. But he does not speak for me and his difficulties and confusions are (I hope!) his own. But I know I come to the surface in places, e.g. in the death of Kurtz. Thus although I enjoyed doing it I found the technical difficulties of the assignment very demanding, since the father had to relate back to his earlier novels without being able to really see the development happening. But I tried to make his approach careful and analytical and worthy of his daughter's interest.

What value, in your opinion, did the writing of this letter have:
(a) for the student?

(b) for the tutor?

Clearly it helped the student to justify his own approach and the tutor to understand the strategy adopted, thus making it more likely that the tutor's comment will be well informed. You will notice that this teacher and this student talk to one another, though they have to do this through writing. How often do you discuss *your* written work with your teacher?

Only *you* can answer. But *do* you make fullest use of your teacher?

You may have complained about a grade. It's easy to get worried about grades, and sometimes that can prevent you from learning and from enjoying the work. It's as well to accept that grading *is* a problem and then try to forget about it.

This student did worry about grades but tried to keep this aspect in perspective. Read part of an earlier letter he wrote to the tutor:

I try not to worry about grades but I am very fortunate in that I don't need to worry since I already have a degree, (*author's note: not in a subject related to English Literature*) but I can see that a person who needed a degree desperately to achieve promotion would do so. I *do* worry however because it affects my 'ego'. I was disappointed that my first essays were not 'B's' but now I am *sure* they were not worth 'B'. Since then I think I can almost grade what I think it is worth and I am absolutely satisfied except that my work on Turgenev seemed to me to have that 'spark' for an 'A' but I realise the line there was very narrow. I would expect the 'A's' to be very, very rare, otherwise they are not as worth having as they should be.

May I just say that I am willing to bet no one has written and said he should have got a lower grading and that your grading is too high!

Certainly, I have enjoyed the course so far and mean to continue doing so, *and* I have learnt a great deal – both about the work and my approaches to it.

Have you ever written to a tutor (or spoken to a teacher) to complain about too high a grade? If your answer was 'yes' your halo should be clearly visible! Try to evaluate yourself honestly, taking into account both the good and the bad.

4 Some Final Comments on this Case Study

The student's attitude is centred on his subject and the ways of presenting it. He is trying to learn from his essay writing, and he seems to enjoy doing this – although he also stresses how demanding it is.

He appears to have the role of assessment in just the right perspective. (Very often students who put assessment to the side, and get on with the job, end up securing the best grades too.) He writes to his tutor on how he has interpreted the question, and why. He keeps in close and friendly contact, not merely sending the essays to his tutor in an impersonal way.

Constructive Learning From Marked Essays

The comments on your essay can take a variety of forms. Here is a fuller list of what your teacher might be aiming at when he comments on what you have written. (This is based on part of a draft unit called *The Roles of the Part-time Staff in the Open University*, The Open University, November 1975.)

● Comments which acknowledge your point of view, or stage of development. (These might just be ticks as in the case study essay.)

● Comments suggesting new ideas, fresh examples, different opinions. (Plenty of these in the case study essay also.)

● Simple corrections of facts, or mistakes (e.g. in spelling). There are none of these in the essay reprinted in this Unit, but you will remember the examples in Unit 4.

● Comments aimed at helping you to make your written expression clearer (and thus also your thought). This was also discussed in Unit 4.

● Comments guiding you to the proper use of evidence, e.g. use of examples, illustrations.

● Comments which evaluate your essay as a whole (on a separate sheet of paper or form, or at the end of the essay itself). These will probably involve the giving and justifying of a grade or mark. They will perhaps indicate how adequate your structure is in general.

● Comments on *detailed* aspects of your structure e.g. repetitions, sentences out of order, muddled paragraphs. (Unit 4 discussed these points.)

● Comments looking back at work you have done earlier, or at difficulties you might encounter in work to come.

Note: You don't need to rely on your teacher for constructive criticism. Your family or friends can also help you by reading your essays. Unit 4 suggested how you might do this to improve your handwriting, but you could extend this to a wider review of your work. You could ask them:

Did you *enjoy* what I wrote?
Did you find it interesting?
Did you understand it all? If not which parts seemed difficult or confused?
Could you follow my argument or theme throughout?
Did I support my ideas fully enough?

You might ask your friends to do this at the stage of the first draft, and use their comments when you write up the finished essay.

There is no separate revision exercise in this Unit – because *everything* you have been doing has been a thorough revision of what you have learnt – but there is an Assignment.

5 Assignment F

1. In Assignment D, question 3, you were asked to choose an essay topic of your own. Write this up now, using as many words as seem to be required. A rough guide would be 1500 words, but your essay may be a little longer or shorter. Work through *all* the stages suggested in the course. Your time on this question will vary according to the topic you have chosen. It could take between three and six hours.

2. What have you learned from the course *as a whole*? Write a paragraph or two on this. You might also say what you feel you have still to learn or to practise more fully. Have the points you made in Assignment A, question 2, been dealt with (see page 9)?

You have now finished the course – except for learning from your returned essay for this Unit. I hope you have enjoyed it and that the work you have done will prove useful in the future. With this in mind, study the postscript on Essays and Examinations.

6 Postscript: Essays and Examinations

In this course you have studied a suggested range of techniques for writing essays – and any other pieces of continuous prose. These have included knowledge, skills, and attitude. If you practise these techniques each and every time you write, they will become as natural as the earliest examples we mentioned, tying a shoelace and boiling an egg.

Your approach to writing essays in an examination should be *exactly the same* as that which you have learnt on this course, except that the whole process is *speeded up* and is *far more concentrated*. Thus you have to:

● Think and write more quickly.

● Choose more decisively.

● Select your material more accurately.

● Write more relevantly.

● Identify the 'key words' and keep to any word limit more exactly.

● Discard more ruthlessly.

● Ask yourself questions more effectively.

● Concentrate your mind *completely*.

I cannot necessarily expect you to 'enjoy' the exam, because the occasion will always put you under pressure, but you will cope far better if you *adopt a positive attitude*. An example will illustrate this: if there is a very difficult question amongst your choice of essays, you should forget it completely and concentrate positively on the *one* you *are* going to do!

There are many detailed guides to examination technique which will help you further (e.g. Lesson 6 of *How to Study Effectively*, Richard Freeman, National Extension College). This postscript is simply making the point that by working through the course, you will have done a great deal *already* to improve your essay writing *for examinations*. However, if you think you need more practice, then I suggest you do again some of the Assignments on this course (or others set by your teacher) under exam conditions, and above all set yourself *an exact time limit* (and stick to it!). You have been encouraged throughout to limit yourself to a maximum period for each task; your work under exam conditions will be a more disciplined extension of this idea.

DISCUSSIONS

Unit 1

1.1 Discussion

Here are some of the things you may have put in your answer:

Knowledge: you need to know *how long* the egg takes before it is ready (and other things like how to operate the controls of the cooker).

Skills: manual skills, e.g. being able to get the egg out of the pan without scalding yourself.

Attitude: you must want to do it in the same way as you *wanted* to tie the shoelace.

1.2 Discussion

Here is my own list. The comments in italics relate these activities to the language of essay questions.

● Discussed different grades of petrol with mechanic.

*Essays often get you to **discuss** in this way, sorting out perhaps one thing as being better or more important than another.*

● With my neighbour's help, worked out a list of the repairs to be carried out by the builders of my new house.

This is rather like the 'outline' type of question – we 'outlined' in our conversation all the things to be done. Later we made a written list.

● Swapped jokes with my brother about teachers we both knew.

This could have formed the basis of a relaxed informal essay of the 'Write about the time when you . . .' kind.

1.3 Discussion

You may have found this quite difficult. I hope, though, that you managed to get the essence of the spoken encounter. Here's my dialogue; you can compare it with yours. I am directing a passer-by from my house to the nearest Post Office.

Man: 'Excuse me.'
Me: 'Yes!'
Man: 'Could you tell me the way to the nearest Post Office?'
Me: 'Yes, you go up there.' (Points up the road.)

Man: 'Up there?' (Turns to face up the road.)
Me: 'Yes, carry on up for a few hundred yards. It is up a turning on the right.'
Man: 'On the *right*?' (Emphasises right.)
Me: 'Yes, – let's see, – it's not the first turning but I think it is the second. It's a few hundred yards up and you'll see a big private hotel on the corner. It's a bit run-down looking, with a red gnome in the garden.'
Man: 'How long should it take me?'
Me: 'Oh, about 10 minutes I should think. Turn right by the private hotel and then it's on your left – a hundred yards or so.'
Man: 'Thanks a lot!'
Me: 'Are you new here?'
Man: 'Yes – trying to find my way around!'

1.4 Discussion

One important difference between speaking and writing is that when two people are talking they have more than just the words to help convey their meaning. What sort of things? Think about this for a moment. Gesture and facial expression are two very important aids. Hence, in my example, there was a fair bit of pointing and turning going on – physical acts which are quite impossible when you are trying to explain things to someone on paper. Then again, if the speaker sees, by looking at the person he is talking to, that a direction is not clear, he can always either repeat it or put it a different way. Hence, in my example above, the man could interrupt every so often, in order to understand the route fully.

Notice too the way the voice can quite easily convey emphasis ('on the *right*'). Also, spoken communication is always made easier by words and phrases that do little more than establish a friendly kind of social contact, e.g., 'Yes – let's see . . . I think . . . a bit run-down looking . . . oh . . . I should think . . . Thanks a lot.'

1.5 Discussion

Here is my attempt.

With 92 Stockton Lane on your right, go up the road, leaving the town behind you. Go past the first turning on your right until you reach a private hotel standing on the corner of a turning. Turn right there, and you will find the Post Office about one hundred yards down on your left.

1.6 Discussion

In the written communication:
(a) Fewer words are used. We have to select more carefully what it is we want to say.

(b)   There is greater precision in it, too. This is because the *words* are all the reader has to go on. The meaning has to be absolutely clear. It is important to remember this when writing essays; you can't rely on the reader guessing your meaning: it must be there on the page.

(c)   Punctuation has to be careful and exact. Try deleting all the punctuation from the written example and see how confusion could easily occur.

(d)   It is rather more impersonal; there is less friendly padding (or none at all). It is not easy to establish a friendly written style which is also exact.

(e)   The directions have a kind of form about them. They start and finish, the details are welded together, and there is a sequence of logical steps between them.

(f)   Any emphasis – e.g. of tone or gesture – has to be conveyed through vocabulary, sentence rhythm, or punctuation.

(g)   One point not immediately obvious, but very important, is that we can turn to written words at any time: they endure. Spoken words fade as soon as they have been said. A reader can take his time over understanding what has been written; he can choose his own pace. Hence, writing can be much more *concentrated* that speech; the reader can look back over it, return to it, think about it, check it.

Spend a minute or two looking over these points, along with any others you have made. They are important.

Unit 2

2.1   Discussion

The first is **French** (from *Living French* by T. W. Knight, ULP, 1952, p. 116).

The second is **maths** (from *Modern Mathematics for Schools* Bk. 3, Scottish Mathematics Group, Blackie & Chambers, 1972, p. 43).

The third is **biology** (from *Introduction to Biology* by D. G. Maclean, Murray, 1962, p. 10).

I think you will agree that the language, as well as the subject matter is distinctive. This is partly because each 'subject' looks at different aspects of the world we live in and asks different questions about it. Geography, for example, looks at land surfaces, while maths looks at the relations between numbers. (Both also look at other things too, of course.) Each has its own special terms, such as 'reflexive', 'verbs', 'perfect tense' and 'past participle' from the first extract.

2.2 Discussion

The passages were aimed at the following readers:

(a) Children. (The extract is from *Puffin Post*, Vol. 5, No. 1, 1971. It is intended for children of about 8–14.)

(b) Parents. (This one is from a pamphlet produced for parents, to help them to develop their children's language.)

(c) Teachers. (The extract is from a book called *Reading Together* by Kenyon Calthrop.)

(d) A general audience. (This is from an article in the *Radio Times* about Frances Hodgson Burnett, 2nd January 1975.)

(ii) (a) is simply written, with quite short words. It appeals to a *child's* interest in magic.

(b) is written for an adult, though you might not necessarily have said 'parents'. It could, for example, have been written for those whose jobs bring them into contact with children, such as nursery nurses.

(c) seems angled at teachers, or at those who train them. The matter of whether or not Drama should be a separate department in school gives this away. The language is much more involved than in (a).

(d) You might not have got this. It's fairly typical, though, of writing which aims at interesting a wide section of the population. Think of all the people who might pick up the *Radio Times*.

2.3 Discussion

The first piece is full of lively detail, trying to convey a scene of bustling activity. The second is written from a position of greater detachment: the reader in mind might be a motorist driving through and wondering whether or not to stop in the village.

2.4 Discussion

(i) is clearly analytical (a history essay); (ii) is creative, expecting the writer to make up a story. Similarly, (iii) is creative (it could be 'made up' or from actual experience). (iv) is rather trickier – basically analytical, though with an element of the creative too. (v) is ambiguous. It would depend on the context – e.g. whether it was an 'O' level English essay, or from an Open University Sociology course. If the former, you would expect a more informal and less analytical approach, rather than explicitly sociological treatment. (vi) is creative (you will soon be practising writing one like this). (vii) is analytical – your own *feelings* about the way land is used would not be relevant.

2.5 Discussion

In the first example the student is asked for personal experience, but he has given instead a very general semi-factual account.

Instead of writing subjectively, he has felt he must be 'objective'. This first question insists on the student using the word 'I'. Did *you* use 'I' and 'me' in your own opening? If not, was it because you felt shy, and felt that you shouldn't be so personal?

The second essay requires a detached analysis and the student has again answered inappropriately. It's a promising opening, but for another kind of question altogether! (In fact, it could develop into an answer to the first question, on Fear!)

Your own answer to the second essay should have shown an ability to stand back and look at *causes* – not events, or results, or anyone's specific experiences. (A good opening sentence might be 'Of the many possible causes, the rise of nationalism seems the most important.')

We shall look later in the course at the importance of analysing the specific words of each question you are asked.

2.6 Discussion

(a) The title asks for a personal account ('my . . .'). This puts it firmly into the creative category. It also gives the writer quite a lot of freedom, e.g. he could have chosen his first day at work. (It's also worth saying that essays like this don't have to be strictly factual. You are not reporting in a court room! You are at liberty to 'colour' the experience if you wish.)

(b) I find it interesting, and I think that is relevant to judging its success. Such an essay should hold the reader's interest throughout (any essay should, but it is especially important here). The student does this partly by a good use of detail – e.g. the badge. (See (e) below.)

(c) 'flash suit . . . holey jumper and holier jeans', 'umpteen pairs of . . . eyes' are all examples of colloquial language.

(d) This use of the colloquial is a strength, I think. It's appropriate to the situation being described: the boy would say 'holey' he wouldn't say 'jumper with holes in'. Or rather, that wouldn't be nearly so vivid. ('A jumper with holes in' would be more appropriate on *other* occasions, e.g. when writing to the headmaster about a fight your son has had on the school premises.) Remember what we said earlier about the way our style varies to suit our purposes and the audience' for whom we are writing.

(e) I liked it. We feel exposed, with the boy. It's lively. The use of 'the badge' is especially good. The writer builds up the tension through dialogue, and delays telling us the motto until we too are puzzled by the question 'Do you?' Then when we see what is happening, we laugh. Similarly, with the art teacher whose behaviour is unexpected. (I'm not saying that it is a perfect piece of writing. The description of the master in the paragraph beginning 'Our next lesson was Art' seems to me overdone. But it is, on the whole, a good essay.)

2.7 Discussion

I don't think this pupil is involved with his topic. He seems to be writing at secondhand providing a rather artificial treatment which he feels will score him high marks. Look at the over obviousness of 'trips', 'its merry way' and 'little children'. There is no real sense of communication with a reader.

2.8 Discussion

The words in italics are those you should have underlined.

Apply the paste *thinly.*
Plant the shoots *at intervals of 3 inches.*
Mix the powder *with a little water.*
Use blank cartridges.

Notice that 'paste', 'shoots', 'powder', and 'cartridges' are content words (see the comments about these earlier in this Section). The words we have underlined are those which tell you what to do with the things, how to treat them. They give you essential information as to *how* you should carry out the necessary task. You would be a fool if you ignored them: you would waste money, or time, or even endanger life. Yet students very frequently ignore the key words in their essay titles.

2.9 1. Discussion

You should have underlined *Assess.* It is the word which tells you how you are expected to write about the causes. (Another significant little word is 'main'. You are not expected to enumerate every possible cause, only the *main* ones.)

2. Discussion

Narrate, Explain, Describe and *Tell* are the key words. Notice, also, how 'main' and 'principal' come into the first two questions. Now we'll try an example that is much more complex, but whatever your intended level of study you should be able to recognise the key words without much difficulty.

3. Discussion

Obviously, all the words are important. But for the first question I underlined: *possible, differentiate, different, disciplines* and *subject matter.* 'Differentiate' and 'subject matter' seem to need double underlining!

For the second questions you should have underlined: *power, social scientist, analysis, patterns, social conflict* and *validity.* 'Patterns' and 'social conflict' need double underlining.

2.10 Discussion

Student B is directing his work intelligently to the actual

question. He is thinking ahead and he will probably get much further than student A, in much less time.

2.11 Discussion

Anybody should be able to have a go at asking questions using commonsense. Below are a few examples of the questions to which I should look for answers.

(a) What is volcanic activity? What area – where? What kind of problems? How far from volcano? What kind of living: physical safety? growing crops? working?

(b) How many steps? Why did he want to 'pacify' Ireland? Why was Ireland angry? Was it all of Ireland, or only parts? What sort of measures did Gladstone take: physical force? Acts of Parliament? discussion with Irish leaders? economic aid?

(c) Isn't Milton a 'great poet'? Is the critic trying to be rude about him? How does a bricklayer lay bricks?

(d) How is 'attitude' being used here? What are some examples of attitudes? Do *I* have attitudes? If so, what functions do they serve for me? Is 'functions' being used in a particular way in this question?

(e) Do they have a different God? Or the same God viewed in a different way? Why do they disagree?

(f) What kind of classroom? What kind of 'order'? Is 'order' the same as 'discipline'? What exactly are 'educational psychology' and 'educational sociology'?

You could of course go much further, and ask questions about your questions, or work out possible answers before you turn to your books. In any course you did, you would also be more specific in your questions since you would be familiar with parts of the subject already, e.g. a concept like 'function' would already be clear to you from your previous work.

Unit 3

3.1 Discussion

A seems to be setting about his task in a much more systematic fashion than **B** – though we would need to see the complete essays before we could be sure. **A** is defining his terms, and showing that he has spotted important words in the question and their possible implications. What **B** says is sound enough, but it is rather jumpy and abrupt, as if he's thinking it all out for the first time as he goes along.

The opposite fault is *heaviness* in introductions – ponderous statements which say little and seem to be 'warming up'.

3.2 Discussion

This introduction takes a very long time to say very little. It may seem impressive, using phrases like 'a consideration of the above mentioned proposition' (long words!) and 'the school situation' (jargon for 'school'). But it says little, and it doesn't catch the reader's attention.

3.3 Discussion

Here is my attempt:

Sentence 1. I'm not sure whether or not this book is suitable for use in school.

Sentence 2. Especially as I have only just read it.

Sentence 3. The detail in it is certainly authentic.

Sentence 4. But this could be the problem!

Sentence 5. So we must look carefully at the issue I raise above.

Even simplified like this, is it a particularly good opening? Is it good to start by confessing your own uncertainty? You might have underlined the whole of the last sentence and cut it right out. The student is writing in a ponderous way.

3.4 Discussion

Here is the order in which they actually appeared (in *Protect Your Home*, Central Office of Information, 1975):

> If you're going on holiday, ask a neighbour to keep an eye on the house and report anything suspicious to the police. Ask him to remove any circulars or anything else that might advertise your absence. You might even get him to cut your grass – yet another give away for the thief. Of course your neighbour would expect you to do the same for him! Tell the police when you are going away and also whether your neighbour has a spare key.

No *one* order is 'correct', though you should make sure that your order makes sense. In the muddled version, for example, we don't know who 'him' refers to in the first sentence.

Look back to Unit 3, question 5 (page 37) and notice how – particular in examples (a) and (b) – the first main sentence really has to be at the start of each paragraph.

3.6 Specimen Answers

A. Born on 20th August 1873, Jones by 1906 was regarded as a rising politician. Yet, although the Prime Minister in 1909 credited him with being 'the true progenitor of the Labour Exchanges Act', he never achieved office, and in fact he faded out of politics during the First World War. The key may lie in his private life: married in May 1903, he was divorced eight years later; his household accounts suggest that he was a heavy drinker.

B. Jones was born in 1873. He married in 1903. Between 1905 and 1915 he appears to have consumed ten bottles of brandy a week. In 1906 he was regarded as a rising politician. In 1909 the Prime Minister referred to him as the 'true progenitor' of the Labour Exchanges Act of that year. He never achieved office, and faded out of politics during the First World War.

C. Jones, according to the then Prime Minister, was 'the true progenitor of the Labour Exchanges Act' (of 1909). His household accounts suggest that he was a heavy drinker. In 1906 he was regarded as a rising politician. He was married in 1903 and divorced in 1911. He never achieved office and faded out of politics during the First World War. He was born in 1873.

Discussion

A is obviously the best of these three passages: it is clear, orderly, and it reads smoothly. **B** is not so good, though it is preferable to **C** which is very bad as a piece of communication. The faults of presentation in **B** and **C** will be discussed below when we turn to *form* and *structure* in historical writing.

Looking closely at **A** you will note that even in so short a piece of historical writing as this it is practically impossible (and probably not desirable) simply to 'report the facts'. The phrase 'the key may lie in his private life' is a cautious one, but it does show the historian introducing an element of *interpretation*. Meantime check your own answer to be sure that it corresponds more closely to **A** than to **C**.

It may be, though, that you have produced a version which differs quite a lot from **A**, yet is equally good as *communication*. In fact there can be no absolute and final way of setting down even the limited information you have discovered about Jones. This is one of the problems in assessing how good you are at history (or indeed how good a professional historian is): there can be no absolute, one-hundred-per-cent guide as to how you should *present* (another word for *communicate*) your material. But the point to remember is that the material must be communicated: in general it is true to say that some ways are better than others for making sure that information is effectively communicated.

History is not primarily concerned with good writing and literary style; but a person who does not present his material in good English has failed to complete his tasks as a historian. In assessing any piece of history (whether a book by a professor, or an essay by a student) there is room for some difference of opinion over how much weight should be given to facts and ideas on the one side, and presentation on the other. But it is always worth remembering that if your presentation is bad, the reader may not be able to follow your facts, however laboriously discovered, or your ideas, however brilliant.

The Basic Elements of Form and Structure in Historical Writing
Passages **B** and **C** in the previous exercise do not communicate a very clear statement about Jones because they are badly organised, they lack form. **C** is particularly weak because it simply sets down the pieces of information about Jones as they turned up, without any attempt to place them in logical sequence. **B** is rather better because it has at least arranged the information in chronological sequence: that is, beginning with his birth and working through the years till his final fade-out from politics. The trouble here is that each fact – important and unimportant – is given equal weight; and there is no attempt to establish any meaningful relationship between different facts. As far as this passage is concerned, one year of consuming ten bottles of brandy a week might be directly related to his being regarded as a rising politician.

Of course, form or organisation is required in any piece of writing, not just historical writing. The point is that facts and ideas thrown together in any kind of slap-dash sequence simply will not communicate themselves to someone else; indeed, disorderly presentation usually suggests that the writer himself is not completely clear in his own mind. To grasp something quickly and firmly, the human mind demands orderliness: it is fairly easy to grasp the contents of a bookshelf in which the books are arranged systematically by subject; it is less easy to do so when the books are crammed in any old how, or even when (as has been known) they are arranged in accordance with the colour of their binding.

In writing, the basic purpose of organisation is to get the emphasis right, to direct the reader away from less important matter, while making sure that he has grasped the really important information.

The difference between the Jones passage **A** and passages **B** and **C** lies in the effort which has gone into **A** to get the emphasis right. In the first sentence, the date of birth is treated rather as incidental, the real weight falling on the positive point that Jones was a rising politician in 1906. From there, we pass in the second sentence to the central point about Jones: he did, in regard to the Labour Exchanges Act, achieve something of true historical significance; but, almost in the same breath as it were, it has to be made clear that that was all he achieved – that in other respects he already seems to have been on the way out. Lastly, with slightly less emphasis, we come to the details of his private life, which through a simple piece of interpretation by the historian are deliberately presented as a possible explanation of his lack of political success.

(Reprinted with kind permission of the author, Professor A. Marwick.)

Unit 4

4.1 Discussion
You should pause between planning and writing up to allow further assimilation to take place; to give the mind a rest before moving on to the final stages. Notice how organisation is important if you are to do this. Writing an essay, from the earliest point (described in Unit 1) to the end product, takes time, which the mind needs to work through the various stages (compare this with a programme on an automatic washing machine). Students who leave all the work till the day before their essay is due to be handed in usually fail to do themselves justice, even though they may be quite good writers.

4.2 Discussion
These are some of the advantages of writing two versions, which you may have listed:

● It gives you more time on the essay and so you might phrase some of the more complex points more tellingly or lucidly.

● You can get your ideas down on paper in the first version and then concentrate on polishing them for the *final* version. That way you need not worry about the accuracy or elegance of your phrasing until the final copy. (One way of setting out your first version is to write on only half the page, leaving the rest for your comments and rephrasings at a later stage.)

● You will produce a much tidier end product: as will be argued later in the Unit, presentation is important.

Now here are some disadvantages:

● What you gain isn't worth the time you spend. Copying it out is laborious, and you might have found a better use for your time.

● Some students worry so much about seeking perfection that they revise the *finished* product, sometimes more than once!

I suggest that you start by allowing time for the *two versions*. When you become proficient, you might be able to dispense with the rough copy stage.

4.3 Discussion

(a) The passage is awkward and unclear. And, most important, *it doesn't succeed in communicating anything*. It is one thing for the reader to need to pause over a profound or complex idea: quite another to have to peer through obscure language to see if there's anything there at all.

(b) I think it means something like:

Paul Morel had the intelligence to make his father's valuable introspection more available to the other members of the family. He could have drawn his father out. This analysis could be said to apply too, to Lawrence's relationship with *his* father.

It is not at all clear what the first part of the second sentence means – 'The total avoidance . . . in his mind' – and you'll have to take my word for it that the context doesn't help either! The first thing the reader has to do here is to work out what the student means. The writer has failed in his responsibility to make his ideas clear, and the teacher is expected to finish his thinking for him. It is no good for the student to say, a week later when they meet in the corridor, 'Oh, but what I really meant to say was . . .' If the point isn't clear in the essay then no credit can be given. No examiner would (even if he could) ring up a candidate to ask him whether what he was trying to say on side 8, question 2, was . .

You can see that the passage given in question 3 is wordy, vague, roundabout, abstract and a bit pretentious. Its phrasing is ambiguous. These are usually sure indications of an inadequacy in the thinking behind the essay.

4.4 Discussion

The original as I first wrote it is as follows:

Of course, in an actual course, you will be able to go farther, since you will realise what kind of question your discipline asks – e.g. if (v) were in a course on Religious Education, you would be alert to the concepts used and the appropriate discourse.

So don't just plunge into a pile of reading. Ask questions to guide your study (and to cut it down!). As you read, you will want to extend and refine your questions, and maybe cross some of your marginal ones out.

Do not be afraid to use other sources than books. There may be useful material in radio or TV programmes (e.g. a radio debate between Protestants and Catholics; a TV documentary about a volcanic area). Casual discussions may be significant too – for these reasons it is a good idea to carry a notebook with you wherever you go. And don't forget to record the sources of your ideas. As we shall see, it is important to attribute the sources of

any quotations you may use in your essay. Record:
author
title
publisher
date of publication.

Here are one or two points to notice about the punctuation in the above passage.

e.g.   – Use full stops, when using abbreviations.

(v)   – Note the use of brackets. (Another way of doing this is by dashes e.g. – v – or commas, v,)

don't   – punctuation to show a missing letter.

!   – a full stop would have served equally well, but an exclamation mark seems to give a chattier tone, more in keeping with the Course; similarly with the dashes – to get the effect of a spoken voice, as much as possible.

:   – after 'Record'. The colon often introduces a list as here.

;   – the semi-colon forms a longer pause than a comma.

For more practice in using these various punctuation marks see *English for the Individual* by Marland and Thompson and *Practical Punctuation* by Ian Gordon (both Heinemann Educational).

Don't forget there's no *one* way of doing this: perhaps you have improved on mine. Did you paragraph as I did? Again there were alternatives, e.g. you may have felt that three paragraphs were too many. But the beginning of the third paragraph does seem to introduce a new emphasis. Some of you may have felt that a fourth paragraph could be started with 'And don't forget to record the sources of your ideas.' On the other hand, too many paragraphs can lead to a disjointed effect.

Finally, this passage was originally a draft for Unit 2. Look at the passage as it is now in Unit 2 (page 23), note the changes I made, and work out why I made them.

4.5 Discussion
Here is my corrected version:

Why a comma?

Why a comma?

✓

It is natural for D. H. Lawrence to include in his writings, life in mining communities, after all he was the son of a miner. 'Sons and Lovers' is not only a novel, about a man coming to terms with himself and the people he comes into contact with, but a story of community life in the late nineteenth century and the early twentieth.

There is an early mention in the first chapter of how mining communities came together, the closing down of the small 'gin pits' and centralisation by big mining companies, building larger mines. It

Choose one of these two words

(:)

awkward

Rather a vague end to a sentence

type
Is this a sentence?

existence

Why a comma?

heavier punctuation around here.
semi-colons?

Why a comma?

was this centralisation, which gave the mining village its own particular way of life. The large companies built houses for the miners, 'The Bottoms' were this type of housing. 'The Bottoms' consisted of six blocks of miners dwellings two rows of three, like the dots, on a blank six domino. It is here where can be seen the true ethos of mining community life, a lifestyle governed by various factors. The closeness of the houses brought people together, they shared each others joys and miseries, they helped each other, they knew each others business.

A tipe of narrow back alleys with ash pits, low walls, women chatting over the back wall, children playing in the backs, and around the front a different world. The fronts of the houses only reflected a neat tidy existance, neat lawns and gardens, neat parlours hardly ever used, a place to go when dressed in ones 'Sunday best'. At the turn of the century this was not every Sunday.

The closeness of the housing helped make a close community, but the one thing, which drew them together the most, was the menfolk, all were miners, they all knew each other's jobs, it was this particular hazardous job, that made the miners true comrades, and put each man working below ground on equal terms. In times of trouble each man would join together and becomes a team in a rescue attempt or in sickness, when Morel was ill his workmates helped with a little cash just to make sure his family would not starve.

Did your comments agree with mine? You will notice that I've concentrated on punctuation. This is because it seems to me that the student's major weakness lies there. It's not so much that she is muddled in her mind; rather that she is insufficiently aware of what a flexible instrument punctuation is. She makes no use at all of the semi-colon (;) or the colon (:).

4.7 Discussion

The quotes are at lines 3; 5/6; 13/14; 18/19; 25/26; 33/34; 36/37; 38–40; 49/50; 55/56. They are brief, well integrated and are evenly distributed throughout. We never lose touch with the student's own argument and analysis: he is using quotations for his own purposes and in the process he is showing his own excellent knowledge of the book.

His structure seems to be a clear one:

paragraph 1. The Smallweed family offers an example of how Dickens reveals the danger of an obsession with money. (Note that the student starts with a good point: there's no, 'To begin with I intend to look at . . .' or 'In this essay I shall . . .'

paragraph 2. The Dedlocks and property. Their connection with Job. (A new paragraph at about line 21 might have helped further here?)

paragraph 3. Further examples of selfishness. (Note that the 'key sentence' in this paragraph is at lines 46–48.)

paragraph 4. A conclusion. Notice there is no 'scaffolding' like, 'Thus it can be seen that . . .'

There are *others* ways, of course, of organising this material, as you may have suggested in your notes. But this student stays relevant throughout, and the essay is interesting and vital.

4.8 Discussion

(a) op. cit. means 'in the work already referred to'.

(b) There is 'b' because Davies wrote two pieces in 1973 and both have been quoted. 'a' and 'b' distinguish the two in the Bibliography.

(c) You might not have noticed this, but the page number would have been helpful – e.g. Field (1968, p. 21).

Unit 6

6.1 Discussion

My key words (or phrases) would be *imagine, year, great reader of novels, difficulties, 'modern' authors, your grown-up children, author unknown, 'Heart of Darkness', write a part of a letter, describing your response to it,* and *1500 words*. Words perhaps requiring *special* attention in this question are: imagine, letter, your response.

6.2 Discussion

Compare your list with the tutor's comments, which are added to the copy of the essay which follows.

My dearest Daughter,

I did appreciate your kind thought in sending me a copy of 'The Heart of Darkness' by Joseph Conrad. As you so often say there is such pleasure in reading and I am delighted that the encouragement I gave you all those years ago has been of benefit. My gratitude is tempered by my disappointment at not enjoying it as much as I had hoped.

I suppose my difficulties began because I was not fully prepared to accept the way the story was told. I have

good

yes, you're on to an important point: the uncertain validity of the narrative as compared to the 19th century certainty (etc.)

We can't know but can only offer interpretation

↓

say why it matters that there is confusion

there's a lot compressed between the two arrows: too much perhaps?

↑

(though the Thames is also supposed to be linked to the Congo) yes!

You don't feel convinced that some of this is possibly ironic? (e.g. of 20th century subtlety)

cf. here 19th century novels of self-discovery, or the different ways they do it.

Well put →

reservations about the style of narration and about the way the narration is 'placed' in another setting. I accept ✓Marlow as the narrator, but I am puzzled as to why Conrad thought it necessary to have another narrator ✓introduce Marlow, and I am certainly unsure of the relationship between the author, the first narrator and Marlow. Since I know little of the first narrator I have no ✓yardstick to judge his comments on Marlow, which should be significant – or should they? After all, it is he who queries whether the meanings of a sailor's story should be internal or external and this does affect my acceptance of Marlow's story. My view of Marlow could be drawn entirely from what he says, thinks and does, (or more accurately, what he says he said, says he ✓thought and says he did!) but I have a constant nagging doubt engendered by the first narrator and by some of the links, e.g. 'Try to be civil, Marlow' (p. 57) that there is more to him that I need to know. Perhaps it is only through a lifetime's familiarity with their work but I believe I can relate and identify Austen, Eliot and Dickens through their control of the narration (though I would be the first to admit that Emily Brontë is very complex in this respect) whereas modern writers <u>seem</u> <u>to confuse</u> the issue. How much about Henry James does Maisie know or reveal? Is it Jude or Hardy that is really 'obscure'? More particularly who is Conrad? Can he achieve distance and perspective by viewing himself as Marlow through the other narrator? Or is it that Conrad as the first narrator is seeing himself in the character of Marlow as he has become through the power of experience, rather than as he was?

This confusion is made worse for me because of the placing of the narrators in the setting on the Thames. I can appreciate that the juxtaposition of its calm and order against the chaos of the Congo does have a dramatic effect but the <u>puzzling anonymity</u> of the five people on the 'Nellie' is in such direct contrast to the details about those on the Congo that unity seems to be lost. In addition there seems a definite (but deliberate) stylistic difference between the attractive past of the Thames – 'ships whose names are like jewels flashing in the night of time' – and the awful present of the Congo, which is, for me, too emphatic to convince.

Although there is a sequence of actions and events which can be called the story it appears that what I am ✓✓being asked to do as reader is not just accompany Marlow in his search for Kurtz, but rather share with Marlow his discovery of himself. In these modern novels there seems to be a need for something <u>far beyond mere</u> <u>reading</u> which I suppose one could call a <u>depth of</u> <u>perception</u> and this demands a great deal from the reader. I am fully aware that Conrad is consciously and

the problem of a
dropping away of
common ground
between reader and
author?

interesting
but define

expand? Make
clearer?

might it be worth
pointing out that a
lot depends on the
way the 'part' is
presented? e.g. Jane
Austen can present a
limited society but
raise central issues of
behaviour and values
(etc.)

good ✓

you raise an
important central
point here – though
you might do more to
clarify the further
implications I
underline

you put this well: the
'blackness' of
insanity? lack of
grasp? uncertainty?

✓ deliberately choosing his words to 'lead me' in a similar way to the authorial comments of earlier novels. The limited length of the book means that, although there are fewer words, more references and meanings are compressed into them, and I am not really sure that I understand all the links and connected ideas. Since I believe that the novel should be capable of standing on its own, I expect the novelist to supply me with all the 'keys' I require.

I think Conrad is seeking to expand horizons not merely in a technical sense but also by examining central themes and placing emphasis on unusual settings. The book does examine the theme of Imperialism (Colonialism!) and suggests that in the clash between Western civilisation and that of Africa there is much that is dubious about the practical realities, irrespective of whatever principles are being extolled. I will admit that most of the earlier novels I admire examine only parts of the society rather than discuss central issues. Perhaps Conrad wishes to make an objective comment on these issues and thus tries to preserve his separateness from Marlow. But the latter is affected – almost overwhelmed – by his experiences and I assume we should be involved too. By his concentration on the limited number of characters Conrad does make it possible for the reader to see the central and broader themes, but it is in the balancing of reality (as identified by Marlow) and the symbolic (as created by Conrad) that I find the greatest difficulty.

Of course symbolism plays an important part in earlier novels but here Conrad by continuous emphasis on, for example, the concept of darkness and evil, may make the reader forget the real darkness and evil that exist. The problem with symbolism is that it may be misunderstood (or not understood at all) and this inevitably means that there are loose ends which I expect the author to tie together. To give one fundamental example: darkness/blackness is found throughout the book. In London (p. 6), by 'those who tackle a darkness' (p. 9), the quarrel over two black hens (p. 12), the black wool for knitting (pp. 15 and 16), 'the jungle so dark as to be almost black' (p. 20), white men with black moustaches (p. 33), and of course many, many others concluding with 'the black bank of clouds' and the 'heart of ✓ immense blackness' (p. 132). But what is this darkness/ blackness? It is not just evil, or the Congo, or Black Africa, or Negroes, or Colonialism, or mystery, or death. It is partly all of these but as I try to perceive it, it seems also to be the areas of the mind that I as reader cannot understand because neither Conrad, nor Marlow, (nor Kurtz) understand them either. One thing that does seem to me to be crucial is the title and the concept of the

'*Heart* of Darkness'. Since the 'heart' and 'life' are in many ways synonymous, is Conrad implying that if we ✓ understand the very spring from which the darkness flows we could understand everything?

I am puzzled – perhaps unsatisfied is a better phrase – by certain other features of the novel. There is a vagueness which seems to have no purpose except perhaps to ✓ create vagueness. Thus the crew of the 'Nellie' are identified by the titles of what they do (except Marlow) rather than by naming them. Similarly 'the Intended' is not identified further though I agree that this ambivalence reminds us of the idealized and idolized concept of Kurtz that she has created in memory of him. There is confusion also in the way we approach Marlow's story, brought about by the comments of the first narrator and phrases such as 'we were fated to hear about one of Marlow's inconclusive experiences' which implies he has told other tales. Is this one out of the ordinary? Marlow himself becomes confused (p. 31) and one must ask if this happens elsewhere.

(some would claim this is deliberate and therefore successful)

expand? ✓
repetition?

you mean in his story?

My final impressions must depend on how I see the death of Kurtz. Marlow believes that Kurtz broke through the heart of darkness 'during that supreme moment of complete knowledge', but he is already ill ✓ himself and his comments on life (are they what he thought or what he is thinking?) are inconclusive. But clearly Marlow (and Conrad) are obsessed by Fate or Destiny – call it what you like – but it is clearly dark to them also. Thus Conrad (with his love of adjectival qualification) reflects through Marlow on life as that 'mysterious arrangement of merciless logic for a futile purpose'. Marlow believes that Kurtz's 'the horror, the horror' is a moral victory, presumably because he has accepted the truth of what he has seen and done. Kurtz is remarkable to Marlow because 'he had something to say and said it' and Marlow shows himself to be truly ✓ ordinary when he lies to the Intended for Marlow does *not* say it. Perhaps the whole conclusion is deeply ironic for surely 'His end was in every way worthy of his life' cannot be interpreted in any other way. Is the reflection of irony present in the listeners on the 'Nellie' who are either overwhelmed or disinterested? Is the final paragraph the ultimate irony in that wherever the 'Nellie' goes, life will lead to the heart of darkness? As you can see your Conrad raises the questions but I cannot find the answers.

as the 20th century novel often is in its central judgements?

(you might complain a bit about Conrad's language!)

Centrally he's pierced the fabric of illusions of normal civilized, social life.

Yes, how are we to take their reaction?

or the right part of myself!

Perhaps when I said at the beginning of this letter that I did not 'enjoy' the novel I may have misjudged my approach. Perhaps enjoyment is only a part of the process and perhaps I did not give enough of myself. I did appreciate the conscious effort and the technical skill of the writing and I do believe the effort to extend the horizons of the novel is to be welcomed. But the difficulties outweighed the assets.

Thank you again for sending the novel. Perhaps it is wrong for me to judge Conrad on the basis of this novel alone but you did ask for my opinion and as you know I am always pleased to give that.

a very patient and understanding father!

Your loving father

6.3 Discussion

(a) He calls it 'creative' in situation and tone and indicates that the 'analysis' was successful in the terms set by the title. The student went straight to 'important questions'.

(b) He suggests that a greater attention to clarity of expression is needed at times, and also that some points could have been more fully elaborated.

6.4 Discussion

(a) Any ticks would do (N.B. there is an overlap between this category and the next.)

(b) *validity of narrator . . ., possibly ironic . . ., common ground . . . .*

(c) arrows and comment *too much perhaps? repetition?; expand; make clearer.*

This list is only a selection from many possible examples and I am sure you have found others too.

Bibliography

This is a list of books which you may find helpful for further work. Some of them have been mentioned during the course, others will be new to you. You are not expected to buy or borrow from the library all or indeed *any* of these books; they are suggested as an optional extra for those of you who wish to improve your techniques further or who have particular difficulties.

Those books published by the National Extension College can be obtained from National Extension College, 18 Brooklands Avenue, Cambridge CB2 2HN.

Section One: Books Helpful on Study Skills Generally

Berry, Ralph, *How to Write a Research Paper*. Pergamon Press, 1966.
Buzan, Tony, *Use Your Head*. BBC Publications, 1974.
Freeman, Richard, *How to Study Effectively*. National Extension College, 1972.
Houlton, Bob, *Carry on Learning*. BBC Publications, 1975.
Maddox, Harry, *How to Study*. Pan Books, 1963.
Parsons, C. J., *Theses and Project Work*. Allen & Unwin, 1973.
Rowntree, Derek, *Learn How to Study*. Macdonald, 1970.

Note: The Berry and Parsons books above are really for working at relatively advanced levels. They go into detail on such things as the conventions of preparing and presenting lengthy written pieces (e.g. dissertations, theses).

Section Two: Books Helpful on Written Expression

Carey, G. V., *Mind the Stop*. CUP, 1958.
Gowers, Sir Ernest, *The Complete Plain Words*. Penguin, 1962.
Jones, Rhodri, *A New English Course*. Heinemann Educational and National Extension College, 1975.
Lewis, Roger, *Wordpower*, National Extension College, 1977.
Lister, T. A., *Writing for Everyone*, National Extension College, 1973.
Marland, M. and Thompson, D., *English for the Individual*, Heinemann Educational, 1964.

Wordpower and *Writing for Everyone* take you through simple exercises to help you write more fluently. *English for the Individual* is useful for correspondence students since it is 'programmed' for individual study. It has sections on such things as punctuation. Rhodri Jones' book, *A New English Course*, is attractively presented and aimed at 'O' level students.

Section Three: Reference Books on Language Usage

Fowler, H. W., *Modern English Usage*. OUP.
Roget, *Thesaurus*. Penguin.
Gordon, Ian, *Practical Punctuation*. Heinemann Educational.

See, too, the various dictionaries suggested in Unit 4:
Chambers' 20th Century Dictionary. Chambers.
Oxford Concise Dictionary. OUP.
Penguin Dictionary. Penguin.
Heinemann English Dictionary. Heinemann Educational.